*The Universe is hostile
to the success of your projects.*

What are you doing about it?

Rainbows & Ratholes:
Best Practices for Managing Successful Projects
ISBN-10: 141964601X;   ISBN-13: 978-1419646010

Copyright © 2006 by Dhanyakumar (Dhanu) M Kothari

All rights reserved. This book, or parts thereof,
may not be reproduced in any form without permission.

First edition: March 2006
Second edition: September 2008

Published in Canada by:

D2i Consulting
58 Aitken Circle
Markham, Ontario
L3R 7L2
Canada
Tel: (905) 475-9285
Kothari@D2i.ca   website: www.D2i.ca

This book is available at special quantity discounts for bulk purchases for corporate promotions, training or educational use. Additional materials including a set of DVDs titled "Project Management Best Practices", customized workshops and project management templates can be ordered from the publisher.

Also by Dhanu Kothari

"From Ratholes to Rainbows:
Managing Business and Project Recovery"
Dhanu Kothari and Romeo Mitchell
ISBN-10: 0978046919; ISBN-13: 978-0978046910

summary of book reviews

Rainbows & Ratholes:
Best Practices
for Managing Successful Projects

"This book about project management is definitely the best down-to-earth guidance I have come across in one place in more than 30 years of reading about, writing about, and doing project management. Whether you are brand new to product development or an accomplished project manager, there is much in this book for you to learn. This book is a best read for all types of project managers."
- *Gerald Mulenburg, National Aeronautics and Space Administration (retired). Review published in the Journal of Product Innovation & Management*

"Provides a spark of insight and energy to nudge a Project Manager over an obstacle or constraint that is hindering the project flow, and the variety of topics covered makes the book timely and invaluable."
- *Earl W. Crisp, D. P. A., adjunct instructor, Mgt. Dept., Univ. of Texas at Arlington and College of Business at Dallas Baptist University*

"Very impressed! You have succeeded in explaining and discussing what is common for all projects no matter what business you are in. I have learned a lot from your book."
- *Olav Bjørnson, Project Manager, Aker Kværner Systems a.s, Norway*

"An invaluable read for anyone who is serious about project & program success! An absolute must read for project sponsors in general."
- *Romeo Mitchell, Senior Program Manager, HP Canada*

The title and cover looked so interesting ... I couldn't wait to see the inside of the book. You have done a marvelous job in writing this book, every word speaks ... and this is the beauty of the book. The language is very simple and easy to understand, sequence of topics and contents also flow very well. Congratulations!
- Syed Ali, President, IT Management SIG, Canadian Information Processing Society

"I really like the structure of the book. Chapters are short. Chapter titles are accompanied by illuminating subtitles. Each chapter starts with a quote and finishes with a Chapter Summary. Each summary concludes with Learning Lessons to Avoid the Ratholes and Best Practices for Catching the Pot of Gold. There is much to like in the book ... Kothari offers good advice and distinctive perspectives throughout his book. Take your time with the book. It will pay off for you."
- Hal Macomber, President, Reforming Project Management

"Glad to see a book written by a passionate professional. It synthesizes huge knowledge and experience of Project Management and the best of ideas in taking project management to results."
- Dr. K. Momaya, Associate Professor, Dept. of Mgt. Studies, Indian Institute of Technology (IIT), New Delhi, India

"Novel take on the angst of a project manager/sponsor. Provides a training framework and is an interesting read."
- Bob McClelland, Director, Transportation & Works., Regional Municipality of York, ON

"Wonderful read! I wish I had this book years ago. Finally there is a book with all the concepts, best practices and examples all in one place. I have already used some of the concepts in the book."
- Tony Josevski, P. Eng., PMP

"Describes the subject clearly and succinctly. A deceptively simply book that takes the reader out of the clouds and plunks him/her down firmly on the ground ... I appreciate the way you consistently nudge people to work together with others, and think ahead. This would be a great book to use as a textbook, in a course with multiple case studies.

- Dr. Michel Desjardins, Professor, Faculty of Religion & Culture, Wilfrid Laurier University, ON Canada

"Well organized and written in plain, generic terms and simple language, appealing to anyone from novice to the well seasoned in our profession. A brilliant piece of work! "

- Bill Geraats, President, VISTA Learning Services

This book is a very handy little publication, packed with good advice – especially for those relatively new to project management and working in information technology related organizations.

- R. Max Wideman, Fellow, PMI

acknowledgements

This book was only made possible with the enthusiastic support of family, friends, clients and colleagues who shared with me a passion for Project Management. Without their constant encouragement, it would have forever remained an "unfinished project awaiting completion".

I am deeply indebted to Romeo Mitchell who provided valuable insight by sharing experiences, challenging assumptions and formulating ideas for this book. Romeo practices what he preaches, and he is truly a role model for Project Managers.

A special thank you to my clients from government and industry organizations and, to the students from Humber and Centennial Colleges in Toronto, all of whom have adopted the various models described in this book and made helpful suggestions to enhance them.

A very special thank you my wife, Neela, for sacrificing her leisure hours to let me work on this project. I also thank my daughter, Priya, for reviewing the manuscript and sharing her enthusiasm for the book. Both of them enriched the content of the book by lending their unique professional perspectives as an architect and a paediatric dentist respectively.

Rajini Comfort patiently reviewed the manuscript and provided guidance during its development and editing. Christine Kwan managed the book design and layout with creativity, dedication and enthusiasm. Thank you Rajini and Christine!

Dhanu M Kothari
Toronto, Canada
October 28, 2007

Dedicated to …..

My wife Neela
&
My daughter Priya

Your enthusiastic support
and encouragement
made this book
a reality.

rainbows & ratholes:
best practices for managing successful projects

Table of Contents		Page
Introduction		1
Chapter 1	The World of Project Management	3
Chapter 2	Responsibility without Authority - The Project Manager's Dilemma	13
Chapter 3	Where is the ROI? - Management's View of the Project	19
Chapter 4	Getting the Baseline Right - The Planning Process: - Activity Vs. Productivity	27
Chapter 5	It's Out of Scope! - The Creeping Elegance Syndrome	35
Chapter 6	Who's Doing What to Whom? - The Actors, the Script and the Storyline	45
Chapter 7	Getting to the Finish Line - The Implementation Roadmap	57
Chapter 8	If it's Not Documented, it Doesn't Exist - The Discipline of Project Operations	67

Chapter 9	Who's on First?	81
	- Delegating Responsibility	
	- Getting Commitment	
Chapter 10	Uncertainty - the Only Certainty	93
	- Project without Risks is a Fantasy!	
Chapter 11	The Cost is the Cost is the Cost	103
	- The Mystery of "Runaway" Projects	
Chapter 12	Quality is What the Client Experiences	115
	- The Product and the Process Go Together	
Chapter 13	People Make Projects Happen	127
	- Don't Let Your Team Run Out of Steam	
Chapter 14	It Won't Happen . . .	135
	. . . if You Can't Communicate	
	- Communication Skills & Tools for Survival	
Chapter 15	Manage Your Soft Skills	145
	- The "How" Goes with "The What"	
Chapter 16	Doing the Right Thing for Your Project	155
	- The Professional Project Manager	
	- Skills & competencies	
Chapter 17	Finish the Job with the Right Tools!	165
	- The Project Manager's Toolkit	

Appendix

a.	Checklist: Evaluating Project Mgt. and Team Building Maturity	171
b.	Bibliography and Chapter References	179
c.	Recommended Reading	180

Index   182

x

00 introduction

All projects start with the lofty aim of achieving successful completion and catching the pot of gold at the end of the rainbow. Some, however, fall by the wayside and get lost in a rat hole. Why?

We are faced with Project Management in almost everything that we do, locally and globally, whether we know it or not. In our day to day lives, projects encompass most of our endeavours such as exploring space travel, constructing nuclear power plants, building water filtration systems, conducting heart bypass surgeries, rolling out complex computer systems, managing election campaigns, completing mergers and acquisitions, and launching new products and services. Projects enable us to translate our vision into reality.

Project management plays a significant role in the global economy where the success of international co-operation and world-wide trade depends on projects that are delivered on time, within scope and under budget and that ultimately meet the test of customer satisfaction. To a large degree, our success is associated with managing successful projects.

We can only succeed in projects by embracing project management as a multi-faceted discipline which requires a unique set of skills and competencies to succeed. The purpose of this book is to bridge the gap between the theory and practice of project management by presenting proven and practical guidelines that can be immediately applied for successful management.

This book is organized as a series of essays on the "what and how" of successful Project Management, each one dealing with a specific and practical aspect of Project Management. The essays serve as windows into the world of Project Management and present an integrated panoramic view of challenges and best practices. It is my sincere hope that professionals at all levels and in various functions of management including executives, engineers, project managers, systems analysts, client representatives, team members and students of Project Management will find this book useful.

Successful organizations embrace a "projectized" culture that is founded on the principles of customer focus, committed sponsorship, trusting relationships, outstanding teamwork and continuous improvement. This culture permeates throughout the organization and empowers project teams to operate most effectively and deliver successful projects.

Avoid the rat holes and catch the pot of gold at the end of the rainbow with the ideas described in this book. Here's to managing successful projects!

01 the world of project management

"The Universe is hostile to the success of your projects. What are you doing about it?"

In most organizations, Project Management is practised on an exception basis. We only think of it seriously when the project is in big trouble. The need for Project Management, and in some cases, even its existence, is acknowledged only when we are squarely faced with the reality that the project is out of control.

Our responses to runaway projects are typical. We rely on the magical power of quick-fixes in the middle of a crisis. Typically, we reorganize the project team, seek a change in the design, bring in a new management tool, or fire the project manager and hope for the best.

We tackle the challenge looking for a "silver bullet" and rely on it with a false sense of confidence, only to find that the cycle repeats itself. Faced with problem projects, management soon realizes that controlling them becomes the primary focus of their efforts, instead of running the business itself.

Implementing quick-fixes in lieu of formal project management is like sending a novice pilot on a flying mission. With little training and experience, the pilot is expected to learn the fundamentals the hard way, in the midst of a crisis, and to fix the problems while the plane is still up in the air! Surely, we cannot succeed with this approach, be it with flying or project management.

In both cases, to be successful, it is imperative that there is a clear definition of the mission, roles, responsibilities, plans, contingencies, and rules of engagement. More important, the actions and responses of the participants to ever-changing situations must occur intuitively and confidently. This can happen only with sustained training, comprehensive methodology, rigorous discipline, and growing experience which are the foundations for building professionalism in any discipline.

Despite the vast body of research and awareness of Project Management, the gap between the theory and practice of Project Management continues to exist - resulting in a significant number of failed projects. The gap starts with a lack of understanding about Project Management.

What does a Project Manager do?

"So, you are a Project Manager! What do you exactly do, by the way?" is a comment I have often encountered from my family, friends, professionals and managers. That's easy, isn't it? We plan, coordinate, schedule, control and execute projects. That's all there is to it, you say.

If that is the case, then why do many organizations and professionals continue to struggle with Project Management? Why do so many projects fail while relatively few succeed? What caused the Challenger disaster and what made it possible to land a man on the Moon and bring him back safely to earth? Why did we have the disappointing results of the Concorde in spite of a winning technology, and how did we achieve the impressive success of the British-French Chunnel project? Why are we continually faced with a pattern of failures in IT projects in light of unprecedented progress in hardware and software technologies? The list goes on.

The answers to these questions are varied and complex. However, there is a common thread that weaves them together. That thread is Project Management and it is the basis for success or failure of such undertakings. Project Management is an art as well as a science. It is one of the least understood and least appreciated aspect of management by most organizations.

It is not surprising that, even today, many organizations think of Project Management as just another overhead, full of meetings, administration and paperwork that they can ill afford. It is only in the last 20 years that Project Management has gained recognition as a management discipline and embraced by professionals and academics as a core competency for managing projects.

The Nature of Projects

Let's understand the nature of projects. They are full of uncertainties and risks. If everything happened the way we had planned, if the material arrived on time, if all the resources were available when needed, if the requirements were defined clearly, if the team worked well, if only we didn't have politics in the organization ….. if only!

If everything always happened according to plan, then, of course, there is no need for a Project Manager. But it is in the nature of all undertakings that they are full of surprises, constraints and uncertainties. One of the primary causes of project failure is our ignorance and lack of understanding of what constitutes a project. We seldom worry about the client who wanted the project in the first place. Quite often, we don't even know who the client is!

What is a Project?

Every project has the following ten characteristics. A project:

1. Satisfies a *need* that a business or an organization has
2. Has a *customer* who will benefit from the need
3. Has a *sponsor* who represents management's commitment to the project

4. Has a well-defined *objective* that is directly related to the need
5. Consists of a series of *interdependent tasks*
6. Utilizes various *resources* consisting of men, machines and material
7. Has a specific time frame defined with a *start* date and a *completion* date
8. Involves a degree of *risk and uncertainty*
9. Has an end point or *completion criteria* that defines when the project is done
10. Has the constraints of *scope, cost, time and quality*

These characteristics are also pre-requisites for a project. The failure of many projects can be traced back to the absence of one or more of the above. Such undertakings are hastily started and poorly executed without a proper foundation, a business need, a sponsor, a customer, a risk assessment or completion criteria. It is no wonder that they are headed for the rat hole right when they started.

Unfortunately, the situation gets more complex as many Project Managers don't clearly understand what they are supposed to do. Some think the title itself, "Project Manager", is self-explanatory ….. We manage, we control and we execute.

While many have risen in the organization through the school of hard knocks, some find themselves there as "accidental" Project Managers. Many have theoretical knowledge but lack the experiential base that is so critical to develop as Project Managers. So, what does a Project Manager do exactly?

The Project Manager's Responsibilities

A Project manager is responsible for managing a wide range of functions, commonly known as "Knowledge Areas" as defined by the Project Management Institute. These consist of the following as illustrated in Figure 1.

- ***Control Work Content (Scope Management)***

Project Managers are responsible for managing the scope or work content of the project. Scope Management includes Project Selection, Project Authorization, Project Scoping, Requirements Definition, Project Objectives, Aligning the project with business objectives, and Change Control.

- ***Ensure Timely Performance (Time Management)***

Projects are driven by target dates and schedules, and Project Managers are responsible for completing them on schedule. They achieve this by managing the work for defining, sequencing, estimating, scheduling and controlling the required tasks and activities along with establishing milestones, dependencies and critical path for the project.

- ***Maintain Financial Control (Cost Management)***

Project Managers are expected to complete their projects within an agreed budget. They accomplish this through Cost Management that includes resource planning, cost estimating, cost budgeting, cost forecasting and cost control throughout the life of the project.

- ***Utilize Work Force (Human Resources Management)***

Projects consist of teams and individuals with different backgrounds, skills and expertise. Human Resources Management includes establishing the project organization, defining roles and responsibilities, identifying skills, negotiating for resources, staffing the project, developing internal and external teams and keeping them motivated.

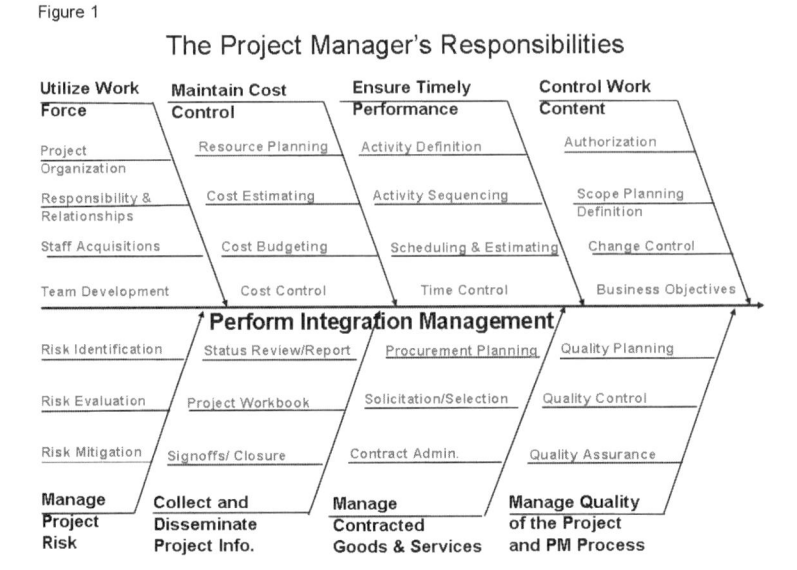

Figure 1

The Project Manager's Responsibilities

Utilize Work Force	Maintain Cost Control	Ensure Timely Performance	Control Work Content
Project Organization	Resource Planning	Activity Definition	Authorization
Responsibility & Relationships	Cost Estimating	Activity Sequencing	Scope Planning Definition
Staff Acquisitions	Cost Budgeting	Scheduling & Estimating	Change Control
Team Development	Cost Control	Time Control	Business Objectives

Perform Integration Management

Risk Identification	Status Review/Report	Procurement Planning	Quality Planning
Risk Evaluation	Project Workbook	Solicitation/Selection	Quality Control
Risk Mitigation	Signoffs/ Closure	Contract Admin.	Quality Assurance
Manage Project Risk	Collect and Disseminate Project Info.	Manage Contracted Goods & Services	Manage Quality of the Project and PM Process

- ***Manage Project Risk (Risk Management)***

Nothing ever goes as planned on projects. Project Managers are responsible for managing risks. Risk Management includes identifying risks, doing an assessment of the risks, developing alternative mitigation strategies, getting management approvals, and managing risks as the project progresses.

- ***Collect & Disseminate Information (Communications Management)***

Project Management is communications! It's the only way a Project Manager gets the necessary work done. Communications Management includes selling the project, managing deliverables, dealing with stakeholders, keeping everyone informed, managing the customer's expectations and getting everyone to achieve the desired outcome.

- *Manage Contracted Goods & Services (Contract Management)*

Projects depend on Vendors, Suppliers and Sub-contractors for goods and services that are purchased from outside. The Project Manager is responsible for planning procurement activities, conducting negotiations with suppliers, administrating project contracts, developing and maintaining contractor relationships, testing and accepting contractor goods and deliverables, and approving payments as work is delivered.

- *Manage Project and Process Quality (Quality Management)*

Quality and everything associated with it influences customer satisfaction. The Project Manager is responsible for managing Quality, both with respect to the project deliverables and the project management process itself. Quality Management includes work related to Quality Planning, Quality Assurance and Quality Control for the project. It also includes continuous improvement of processes for managing projects.

- *Project Integration Management*

A Project Manager delivers successful projects by integrating all of the above-mentioned areas of responsibility. Not one of them can be ignored. Integration Management includes the optimization and integration of all of the above to achieve the intended project outcome and overall client satisfaction.

Who is managing your project?

When you accept responsibility as a Project Manager, you are implicitly responsible for managing all aspects of Project

Management. Understand that you cannot cherry pick your responsibilities and blame the rest on someone else like your management, sub-contractors or team members. As a Project Manager, you are the focal point for the project, and you are ultimately responsible for the success or failure of the project.

Is your project headed for a rat hole?

Ask a simple question, "Whose butt is on the line for this project?" If there is a prolonged silence in the room or an ambiguous response, then rest assured that the project is in trouble. You want a clear, confident and unambiguous response associated with an individual's name, not some department, agency or function in the organization.

Responsibilities ultimately boil down to one individual who is considered to be in sole charge of the situation – whether it be building a house, managing an emergency response, organizing the Olympics, launching a rocket, or even running the office of the President.

Chapter Summary

This is the first window of Project Management. It challenges you to hold a mirror to yourself as a Project Manager and understand your roles and responsibilities. Project Management is about ensuring that you have a valid project that meets all of the criteria, and understanding your role and responsibilities as a Project Manager.

The Project Manager is implicitly responsible for managing all of the nine aspects of Project Management while focusing on "Getting the job done". The lack of understanding regarding the "How and What" of Project Management, both at the management and the individual level, is a major contributor towards project failure. The universe is hostile to your projects. What are you doing about it?

Learning Lessons

Avoid the Rat Hole – Warning Signs

1. Senior Management doesn't believe in Project Management

2. Project Management is on the back burner in the organization

3. "Just do it" is the normal or accepted practice for doing projects

4. There is no distinction between projects and operational or ongoing work

5. No one knows who is responsible for the project

Catch the "Pot of Gold" - Best Practices

1. Understand the ten characteristics of a project

2. Validate that your project satisfies the criteria for each characteristic

3. Understand and internalize the functions of Project Management

4. Establish the Project Manager role as the single point of responsibility for the project

5. Promote and adopt formal Project Management practices

02 responsibility without authority

- The Project Manager's Dilemma

"Project authority …..
You've got it only if you think you've got it."

The concept of responsibility brings up another interesting point. How can a Project Manager be responsible for the outcome of the project if he/she has no authority over resources and decisions in the organization? After all, there are very few people who report directly to the Project Manager. This is common occurrence with a matrix organization. To complicate matters further, none of the other players have a direct reporting relationship.

"They've given us all the responsibility for the project, but minimal authority over what we need for the project ….. Responsibility without associated authority!" is the common lament of Project Managers. Well, folks, I have news for you! You will never have the authority you wish you had, but you will always have the full responsibility for the project. In fact, the reason you have been asked to be the Project Manager is usually because of your skills and ability to manage this dilemma.

The perceived lack of authority seems like a valid argument to begin with. But let's look deeper into reality. How often do you see a project where you have authority over all the factors associated with the project? Consider a simple example of remodelling your kitchen or renovating the basement.

You decide upon budget, draw up a plan, select the cupboards, order the material, hire a contractor and sign the contract. Guess what happens next? The delivery of cupboards is delayed, you knock down the drywall and find a gaping hole, and you have to do electrical work that you didn't expect. The project will now take three months instead of the one month that you had planned, you are living out of a make-shift kitchen in the basement, and everyone including the spouse and the kids are talking about this "Project from hell". You never know what's behind the walls until you knock them down; and such is the case with projects!

The Project Manager's Dilemma

Come to think of it, you have little direct authority over the things that are beyond your control. And that's not just limited to kitchen renovations. It applies to every single project from launching a space rocket, marketing a new product, implementing a computer technology or rolling out a new service for your customers. The scale and complexities of the projects may differ, but the fact is that you have little authority over a vast range of activities that are essential to the success of your project.

In light of these circumstances, what should a Project manager do? The first step is to recognize and acknowledge this reality in the world of Project Management. You will never have the authority you need or deserve, but you will always be accountable and responsible for the project. As a Project Manager, you are expected to work under these constraints, deal with issues and circumstances that are outside your control, and succeed. Who said Project management was easy?

Project Management is the art and science of getting work done with the active cooperation of everyone you need to make your project a success. Knowing the art and science well, and practicing it diligently will make you an outstanding Project Manager. As a Project manager, you have all the authority you need, to do the right thing for the project and your client. The Project Manager's authority is implicit, it goes with the job, and it is expected that you exercise it to get the job done. A big part of this is managing customer expectations.

How do you get the work done?

When I was a novice Project Manager, I often wished that I could carry a baseball bat to the office, swing it and let people know about its existence just in case they don't deliver on their commitments. Or, perhaps, settle such issues with a one-on-one confrontation in the parking lot. However, this is not the ideal way to gain people's commitments or to drive projects.

The only thing you have at your disposal is the ability to effectively communicate with everyone including your clients, stakeholders, team members, executives, engineers, and sub-contractors. Communication involves knowing when and how to use the different tools for communication including written, verbal and presentation skills.

Figure 2
Project Management Roles and Languages

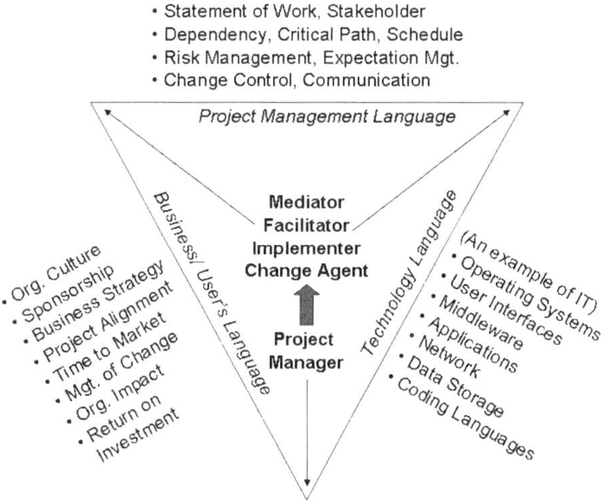

- Statement of Work, Stakeholder
- Dependency, Critical Path, Schedule
- Risk Management, Expectation Mgt.
- Change Control, Communication

Project Management Language

**Mediator
Facilitator
Implementer
Change Agent**

Project Manager

Business/User's Language:
- Org. Culture
- Sponsorship Strategy
- Business Strategy
- Project Alignment
- Time to Market
- Mgt. of Change
- Org. Impact
- Return on Investment

Technology Language (An example of IT):
- Operating Systems
- User Interfaces
- Middleware
- Applications
- Network
- Data Storage
- Coding Languages

In fact, the trick to getting work done is to know first and foremost how to excel in communication skills. Outstanding Project Managers spend 70%-80% of their project time and effort on activities that are generally related to communication. They serve as nerve centres for projects by keeping communications channels open for collecting, analyzing, processing and disseminating needed information and decisions. They know how to delegate and provide the discipline, environment and motivation so that the work assigned to others is completed as expected.

Projects also involve implementing a change somewhere in the organization. Every time a change is introduced, it is bound to affect people, processes and associated technologies in the environment. The change may be as simple as introducing a new form or as complex as merging two companies and changing the culture of the organization. The fact is that human beings resist the very idea of change, regardless of its nature and impact. As such, the Project Manager is responsible for identifying, explaining and selling "the change" successfully so that it is embraced enthusiastically by those affected by it.

The Language of Project Management

Effective communication requires using the right language, and terminology that is clearly and easily understood by your team. That includes the language of Project Management, the language of your business or organization, and the language of the science, discipline or technology related to the project. Figure 2 illustrates the changing role of the Project Manager and expectations arising from the new role.

An engineer who is focused only on technology, to the exclusion of business perspective and Project Management, will not be able to do a good job as a Project Manager. A Business or Functional Manager with no understanding of technology and Project Management discipline will not shine as a Project Manager. A Project Manager, with no understanding of business strategies, their alignment with the project, and high level solutions or technologies will certainly drive the project into a rat hole.

The professional Project Manager "walks the talk" of Project Management principles, "knows the talk" of systems and technologies associated with the project, and "understands the talk" of business and users who will be impacted by the project.

Chapter Summary

Project Management is about accepting responsibility and exercising authority to get the project done. The role of the Project Manager transcends the traditional distinctions regarding job levels, seniority and organizational hierarchy. It is a leadership role that expects the Project Manager to acquire, direct and motivate the organizational resources to cooperate and perform in the context of the project.

In this respect, the Project Manager has various roles as an implementer, facilitator, negotiator and a change agent. The fundamental set of skills to accomplish this is through communication which is the ability to effectively exercise the necessary skills and drive the project towards its intended outcome.

Learning Lessons

Avoid the Rat Hole – Warning Signs

1. The Project Manager has no understanding of the business

2. The Project Manager lacks "people management" and "relationship building" skills

3. The Project Manager thinks that he/she has no authority for the project, or does not know how to delegate work assignments

4. There is a perception that the Project Manager is not "in charge" of the project

5. The Project Manager role is confused with job levels and organizational hierarchy

Catch the "Pot of Gold" - Best Practices

1. Recognize that you have 100% responsibility and minimal authority

2. Exercise the implicit authority to do the right thing for the project

3. Consult and communicate with all interested parties, and get formal approvals as required

4. Understand and speak the languages of Business, Technology and Project Management

5. Develop the recommended skills and competencies for Project Management

03 where is the roi?
return on investment

Management's View of the Project

*"Somebody wants it, Nobody owns it,
Everybody does it. So, let's just do it."*

Let's open the next window and see what is on the horizon. It gives us a view of the project from the senior management's perspective. It is a simple, straight forward view that gives insight into how management deals with a project.

Management is primarily interested in answers to the following:

1. Why are we doing this project?
2. Who in the organization wants this project to be done?
3. Who is sponsoring the project?
4. Where is the budget coming from?
5. What is the Return on Investment (ROI) for the project?
6. What's the priority for the project?
7. When will it be completed?
8. What are the business risks associated with the project?
9. How will the project help us meet our business goals?
10. Where is the Business Case including a statement of needs and cost/benefit analysis?

Sounds reasonable, doesn't it? I would expect every Project Manager to have good answers to these questions. If they don't have the answers, then the project is in a rat hole. In my reviews with clients, I have found that many projects are often started as a result of someone's pet idea, pie in the sky vision, internal competition or just blind faith without due consideration to the players and issues surrounding the project.

Management Support and Commitment

Organizations undertake projects for many reasons: Reduce cost, increase revenue, improve profitability, restructure management and its responsibilities, or implement a vision. A project requires an investment of the company's valuable time, limited resources and scarce funding for its completion, maintenance and upkeep. In that sense, it can be a considered a "Cost Centre" where the overall objective is to optimize resources and costs in relation to its overall benefits to the organization.

The analysis of these benefits in relation to overall costs provides the basis for project justification and Return on Investment (ROI). The first step towards getting management support is to build a solid business case and project justification in consultation with the Project Manager.

Here's what happens when a project is undertaken without management support, commitment and approval:

1. When projects cross departmental boundaries, as is often the case with enterprise-wide projects, they do not have the necessary commitment or "buy-in" from all the departments.

2. Departmental managers are unwilling to cooperate as they do not have the budget allocated for what is seen as a corporate project. This is especially true of organizations structured around the Line of Business (LOB) concept.

3. The Clients and Departmental Managers do not see value or benefit from the project, or do not trust the organization that is delivering the projects.

4. There is no discussion of potential risks; there is inadequate planning for the risks; or project assumptions are unrealistic or cannot be validated.

5. The organizational and project goals are divergent. Departmental priorities, metrics and performance measurements do not align with project urgency and goals.

The Rationale for Projects

Projects exist to satisfy business needs. The needs arise from an organization's strategies and related business goals – increase revenue, improve customer service, gain market share etc. Each business goal, in turn, spawns a number of related projects designed to contribute to it. For each project, there is a list of project objectives which form the basis for the project scope.

Imagine the flow of communication in this complex scenario. Strategies leading to goals, goals leading to projects, projects leading to objectives, and finally, objectives leading to project scope . . . By the time you are assigned to the project, it has gone through at least five levels of communication, translation, assumptions, filtering, spin and interpretations. That is the nature of organizations.

But, what about the project itself that you are about to manage? A lot gets lost in this process with serious consequences. Here is why: Even under the best of circumstances, assuming 90% integrity in communications, the scope is only 70% aligned with the business goals when you start the project. You are already running behind even before you've begun!

Guess what happens once you start the project - the market changes, the strategic goals are modified, the organization changes and the priorities change. Sometimes, you are back to square one justifying the project to a newly appointed manager. This is where the concept of aligning project outcome with business strategy comes in and it is illustrated in Figure 3.

Figure 3
Senior Management's View of the Project

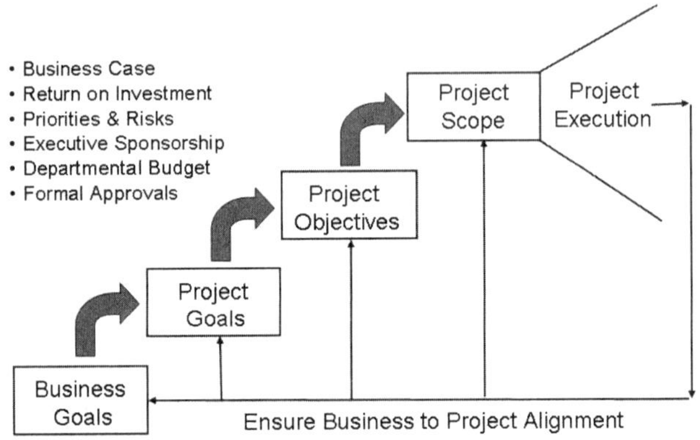

- Business Case
- Return on Investment
- Priorities & Risks
- Executive Sponsorship
- Departmental Budget
- Formal Approvals

Business Goals → Project Goals → Project Objectives → Project Scope → Project Execution

Ensure Business to Project Alignment

The project must be continually aligned with Business Goals and Strategies to ensure management support and commitment.

Project to Business Alignment – The Six Steps

Here is a scenario for a project. Your boss calls you in. "Congratulations! You are the Project Manager", she says. "I know if anyone can get the job done, it's you." What are your chances of completing the project successfully and catching the pot of gold? Pretty good, if you follow these steps:

Step 1: Get the project perspective

Ask questions from a management perspective and get the answers from as many sources as you can. If you are not getting the answers, or if you are getting significantly different answers, then it might indicate a lack of management support and commitment. Quite often, it is a matter of wide-ranging and divergent expectations. Projects with enterprise-wide implementations are a typical example of how managers and departments view the same project differently.

Step 2: Understand project to business alignment

Understand how your project is aligned with the organization's business strategies and goals. Why pursue it, if it is not serving a purpose or if it is not important to the business? The Project Manager ought to know about the client's business, organization culture, business goals and their relationship with the project. Understand the big picture, and how your project fits into it.

Step 3: Sell the Project

Get ready to continually sell the project. Your project is going to affect people, processes, roles and scope of their jobs. People are afraid of change and will resist it. Your success depends on getting everyone's buy-in for, and enthusiastic participation in the project. No one else is going to do it for you.

Step 4: Focus on the Client's Business Needs

Understand and be prepared to articulate the project benefits from a business perspective. How will the project benefit the organization, the customer and the end user? Elevate the discussion from technical jargon to a higher plane that the client can understand.

For example, the project is not just about upgrading the database; it's about satisfying a client or business need for improved customer service. The project is not just about building a water filtration plant; it is about providing safe drinking water to the community.

You cannot expect others to support or believe in your project if you cannot explain the business reason for doing it.

Step 5: Validate & Re-validate Project Objectives

Continually validate the project-business alignment and its objectives throughout the life cycle of the project. The project scope that you agreed to at the beginning may not be valid any more since organizations, strategies and management priorities are always changing. Who do you validate it with? This is where the project sponsor has a critical role: to act as the link between the senior management and the project manager.

Step 6: Apply the SMART Lens

Subject the project objectives through the SMART lens. Are they Specific? Are they Measurable? Are they Achievable? Are they Realistic? And finally, are they Target-driven? Does the scope have an exit strategy? How do you know when you are done? If any of the project objectives fail to meet the SMART criteria, then redefine it with the help of your client to achieve clear answers.

Chapter Summary

Project Management is about continually selling the project from its start to completion. The purpose of a project is to add value to the business or enterprise. It requires an investment of resources and it is associated with costs.

Therefore, a project must be cost justified in relation to its expected benefits, added value to the organization and Return on Investment (ROI). The added value is realized only when the project delivers the expected outcome. Thus, a project is a means to an end, not the end itself.

The famous adage in architecture "Form follows Function" can be easily adapted for Project Management:

Scope follows Objectives, Objectives follow Projects, Projects follow Goals, Goals follow Strategy, and Strategy follows Mission. Thus project scope must ultimately relate to objectives, goals, strategy and mission.

Learning Lessons

Avoid the Rat Hole – Warning Signs

1. No one can clearly articulate why the project is being done

2. The project is suffering from the 3H syndrome – Hype, Hoopla and Hysteria

3. There is no Business Case with ROI justification for the project

4. There are no specific, measurable, achievable, realistic and target-driven (SMART) objectives associated with the project

5. The project direction is not consistent with business priorities and objectives

6. The rationale or business need for doing the project no longer exists

Catch the "Pot of Gold" - Best Practices

1. Articulate the project goals in terms of business needs

2. Continually validate that the project is aligned with the organization's business strategies

3. Set 4-5 major project objectives that have passed the SMART test. Review, redefine and restate the project objectives to satisfy the SMART criteria

4. Ensure that key players associated with the project have a common understanding of its goals and expectations

5. Review, redefine or terminate the project if there is no business need

04

getting the baseline right

The Planning Process - Activity Vs. Productivity

"First Plan the Work, then Work the Plan"

The window for the Baseline Process presents a view of the scheduling process. The implementation of projects starts with a baseline schedule which is just one of the several components of a project implementation plan. A baseline is the first commonly agreed approach among all the players for executing the project, and it takes into account the scope, available resources, internal and external dependencies, project constraints, risks and costs. How do you produce a baseline schedule that is realistic and achievable?

More often than not, the common tendency is to bring up an automated electronic scheduling tool on your computer, and start creating the baseline. Just enter the activities, estimated hours or days, resource names, costs and dependencies and bingo ….. there you have it, the baseline in less than two hours! This is the most favoured approach by mediocre Project Managers, and it lays the ground work for a rat hole into which the project soon disappears.

Can you imagine spending less than half a day on planning a project that ultimately costs millions of dollars to the organization? This is what's known in the industry as the "Fire, Aim, Shoot" syndrome which confuses activity with productivity. We are under so much pressure to deliver that we don't have time to plan! We rely wholly on the latest Project Management tool and pretend that it is going to do the thinking for us. Once the schedule is produced, we just print off a whole bunch of schedules and charts, distribute them to all and let the tool drive the process.

Let us remember that it is just a tool. If tools, templates and forms were all that are needed to run a project, then we wouldn't need Project Managers at all. But projects don't happen that way. There is a proven process for creating a project baseline. Follow it and aim for the pot of gold!

Baselining the Schedule – Ten Steps

1. Establish the Business Need (Strategy, Goals and Objectives) – This should indicate the reason for doing the project, the goals that have been set and the SMART criteria associated with the project objectives as discussed earlier in Chapter 3.

2. Prepare a Statement of Work (SOW) – The basis for the SOW is a good requirement definition. The requirements for the project are stated in simple, clear, unambiguous terms and they are independent of the technology that will be used in the solution.

3. Define the high level solution including a recommended solution approach, components of the solution, sources for acquiring the components (e.g. internally or externally), and a Request for Proposal (RFP) for the components to be sub-contracted.

4. Plan the work and activities to accomplish the project including project definition, Work Breakdown Structure (WBS), Work Packages and Activities. The WBS is an organization chart of the project components that are defined to a manageable level called work packages. More details follow in the next chapter.

5. List the activities for each work package and identify the sequence, dependencies and deliverables for each activity and dependencies. Dependencies help us to identify the order in which we plan to carry out the work. For example, we need a script before we make the movie; we need the patient to be prepared before the actual surgery, and we need to pour the foundation before we build the walls.

6. Establish major milestones for the project. Milestones are points or events in time. Select milestones at 2-3 week intervals that represent significant progress and achievement on the project. List, organize and display the major activities associated with each milestone. This is called the dependency chart. It is a visual representation or a model of how the project will be done.

Figure 4-A

Developing the Baseline Schedule

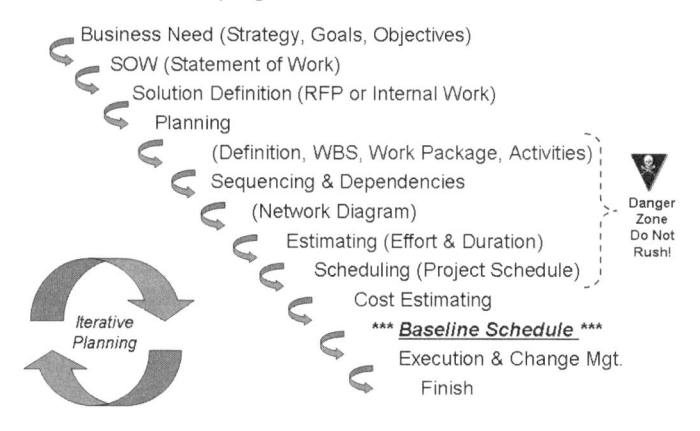

Business Need (Strategy, Goals, Objectives)
SOW (Statement of Work)
Solution Definition (RFP or Internal Work)
Planning
(Definition, WBS, Work Package, Activities)
Sequencing & Dependencies
(Network Diagram)
Estimating (Effort & Duration)
Scheduling (Project Schedule)
Cost Estimating
*** *Baseline Schedule* ***
Execution & Change Mgt.
Finish

Iterative Planning

Danger Zone
Do Not Rush!

Follow the process to "Baseline" the schedule, then
Use automated tools to execute & monitor the schedule

7. Estimate the effort and duration for each activity. Make reasonable assumptions for timing, availability and quantity of resources, technology and equipment. Break down the activities

into durations of 1-2 weeks. Our ability to estimate with a reasonable degree of confidence is pretty good over a range of 90-120 days. Anything beyond that should be associated with a confidence factor of 70-90% depending on the type of project.

8. Finalize the schedule based on time, resource and budget constraints. This will require iterative planning, refining the chart and a review of alternative strategies for fast tracking the project. Provide facilitation to ensure good team input. With effective facilitation, three iterations are more than adequate. They will cover 95% of the needs.

9. Select a strategy that makes the best sense for the organization and the client, and develop the schedule based on estimated resources. There are risks involved with any strategy. Estimate cost based on the schedule, prepare a budget with run rate, and allow for estimated costs associated with risk management.

10. Now you are ready for the Baseline Schedule. Prepare the final schedule and transfer it to an electronic project scheduling tool. You are ready to use the tool of your choice and its functionality effectively.

Figure 4-A illustrates the iterative steps for creating a Baseline Schedule and Figure 4-B summarizes the Baselining process in a flow chart.

Yes, . . . but I don't have time to plan!

One of the common problems I have noticed with "Rat Hole" projects is the absence of this methodical approach to project planning and scheduling. The usual pattern is to skip stages 1-9 above and jump straight to step 10, thus trying to do everything at once using some kind of electronic tool or project management software.

The availability and the ease of bringing up the software on your computer screen is tempting, the apparent speed of producing the plan looks impressive, and the stack of paper with charts, timelines and dependencies shows a lot of work ... but, there's no meat in it!

Planning is all about following steps 1-10, not skipping them for the sake of expediency. Planning is difficult: it takes time, energy, patience, discussion, reviews and facilitation. The pressure and the temptation to jump into execution mode is quite high, and the price to be paid can be heavy in terms of project failure and delays.

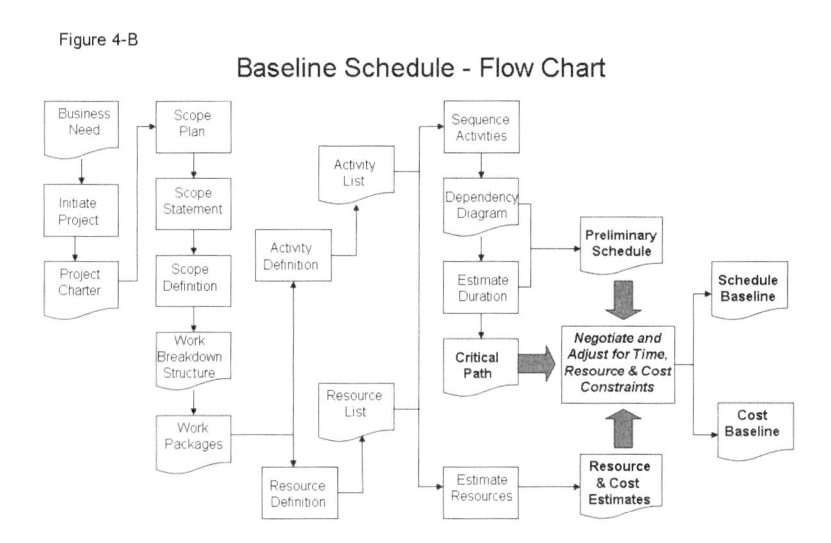

Figure 4-B

Baseline Schedule - Flow Chart

The baseline schedule is a result of the planning process

Planning is an iterative process. It happens on a continuous ongoing basis and takes into consideration the ever-changing dynamics of the project.

A general guideline based on successful projects points to a 20/80 ratio for project planning:

- 15%-20% of the project time/effort is invested in planning and scheduling

- 80%-85% of the project time and effort is spent in execution

Remember, ***proper planning prevents poor project performance***. If you don't take the time to plan and follow the planning process, then you are pushing your project down a rat hole!

Get the Baseline First

A good baseline is the result of team input and intense team discussion. It is driven by a consensus and a common understanding of the project objectives and business needs. It reflects the unique expertise of team members and subject matter experts (SMEs).
The Project Manager's role is to facilitate the process so that the final output – the baseline schedule – represents the team's consensus and a high degree of confidence. After all, what's the use of following a schedule that nobody believes in?

The risks in bypassing the process are that you will never know why the project takes as long as it does, and you won't have the data or supporting material to negotiate for resources, scope changes or risks with your client or management. With a hastily prepared schedule, you will have nothing but unrealistic expectations, a de-motivated team and guaranteed project failure.

Chapter Summary

Project Management is about following a methodical approach to develop a realistic schedule and getting everyone's buy-in. Successful Project managers strip the project to its essential aims, and they break it into smaller, achievable, challenging and realistic milestones. The Schedule is not the Plan; rather, it is a result of the planning process. Failing to plan is planning to fail.

Learning Lessons

Avoid the Rat Hole – Warning Signs

1. Project Management is equated with speed and proficiency in using a Project Management tool

2. The planning process is confused with the "doing" activity

3. Lack of time for planning is an acceptable excuse in the organization

4. There is no team or client involvement in the planning process

5. There is no consensus nor common understanding of the requirements

Catch the "Pot of Gold" - Best Practices

1. Learn and use the three languages of Business, Technology and Project Management.

2. Follow the planning, estimating, scheduling process – the schedule is the final product.

3. Get your team involved in the planning process. There are no tools that will do the thinking for you.

4. Get your client and the team involved in the process. It's easier to get their buy-in and enthusiastic support of the final schedule.

5. Invest time and effort into the scheduling exercise – after all, what's critical is how you arrived at the schedule, not the schedule itself.

05   it's out of scope!

The Creeping Elegance Syndrome

"If you don't have the WBS,
then all you are working with is BS"

Projects are defined by their attributes – scope, cost, time and quality. Scope is at the core of everything in projects, and it is the most difficult to define. The project scope forms the basis for its work content that drives everything else. It answers questions such as:

- "How big is the project?"
- "What are the project objectives?"
- "What is to be delivered?"
- "What drives the specifications?" and
- "What's within the scope and what's outside the scope of the project?

In most cases, the answers to such questions are not obvious, and they are not clearly understood.

Why is scoping difficult?

There are many reasons for this, and we have experienced them all in most organizations:

1. The client doesn't know what he wants and doesn't know what the technology can do

2. The client wants everything and the engineer views it simply as a technology challenge and an opportunity to showcase the latest and greatest technology

3. Sales would rather leave it vague and get the contract signed (let's not forget the cruise!)

4. People make different assumptions about what they are going to get from the project

5. Everyone reads the same document and interprets it differently!

6. The principle of "creeping elegance" works its way through the project - what you are working on isn't the same as what you started with, and you never knew how it happened!

That's the dynamics in organizations. It's real and it's there.

The Project Manager's job is to bring clarity to the project, its objectives and deliverables, and get everyone to agree with them. In spite of the stated requirements and signed agreements, everyone has a different set of expectations and a different view of the project. Although they may have worked on similar projects in the past, no two projects are alike, nor are the Project Managers!

Project scoping helps us to put a frame or a border around the project and then clarify what's inside it. It enables us to deal with ambiguity, and bring clarity to the picture inside the frame. It helps us to break down or decompose the project into manageable chunks of work. Finally, it is about a thought process based on questioning, analyzing and breaking down the work until it produces a cohesive picture of the project.

Ground Rules for Scoping

The scoping thought process is based on two simple ground rules. It relates to understanding the difference between "What" and "How". Our natural tendency is to jump into a discussion of "Hows" rather than understanding the "Whats". We find it much easier to jump into action, start discussing how we will make it happen rather than clearly understanding what it is that we are committing ourselves to.

There is a good reason for falling into this trap. We find it much easier to talk about the details of a wedding rather than the overall scope of the wedding; discuss how we can integrate technologies rather than what exactly the solution would look like; or promise that we can manufacture or market a product rather than talk specifically about its functionality. In short, we love to talk and hear about how we can deliver results rather than what we mean by the results.

The idea of scoping forces us to differentiate the "What" from the "How" of Project Management. It is based on the following principle: Let's define "What needs to be done" before "How we are going to do it".

It Ain't About Solving World Hunger!

There are two other issues that impact the scoping exercise. It is difficult to put a framework around the scope because of interrelated projects and systems. As an example, a project starts with designing a simple web page for customer information, and before you know it, sales expects it to serve as a web-enabled order entry system, and the production folks expect that it will be integrated with the inventory management system, and the finance guys want to see it linked to the accounting system! We all needed it yesterday, so let's go ahead and do it, so goes the argument. This is what I call "Trying to Solve World Hunger!"

Nothing wrong with the expectations, but that's not the purpose of the project although it is tempting to solve all the problems at once. Because of our internal knowledge of the company, and insight into all the problems, we often set too large a boundary for the scope. The Project Manager's job is to set realistic scope for the project, factoring in the constraints and variables of Timing, Resources, and achievable Business Objectives.

Sometimes the project scope is of such breadth, depth and complexity that it might be prudent to split it into separate projects or phases where each one is justified and qualified with respect to the business need. That's why I recommend that projects resulting in major business changes should be implemented in phases with each phase treated as a distinct project.

Techniques for Scoping a Project

The proven technique for scoping a project is known as the **Work Breakdown Structure (WBS).** It is a menu of all the components of a project that is sub-divided to such levels of clarity and granularity that each component can be assigned to a team member and treated as a responsible unit. The commonly accepted definition of the WBS is:

- *"A WBS is a deliverable-oriented grouping of project components that organizes and defines the total scope of the project; work not in the WBS is outside the scope of the project."*
  - Project Management Institute

There are various ways and models in which the WBS can be represented. How you choose to sub-divide the project depends on the way you look at the project, organize it, slice it and manage it. It can be organized by phases, products, sub-components, functionality, organizational units, geographic areas, cost accounts or any other combination thereof.

Choose the model that is relevant and meaningful for your purposes. There is no one right way of looking at the project. Any approach is good. But, there is only one right process for breaking it down. It is the thought process that counts!

Stick to the Nouns and Verbs

The easiest way to build a Work Breakdown Structure is to make effective use of Nouns and Verbs. The Nouns will help you to focus the discussion on the "What". The Verbs will lead you into the "How". At the start of the project, ask "What are the main components?", and follow up with "What are the sub-components?" for each component and so on. Stick to the Nouns to get a handle on the "Whats".

Continue with the thought process until the project work is divided and sub-divided into manageable chunks of work. Stop when you have reached a stage where a component can be estimated with a reasonable degree of confidence and can be assigned to an individual. The lowest level component is called a Work Package and, generally, it should not exceed 2-3 weeks duration.

Each work package then becomes the focus for questioning: "How are we going to get this done?" This is where you start with action-oriented Verbs that lead to activities like Gather material; Draft requirements; Prepare initial design; Get approval; Prepare prototype etc.

From Rock Concert to Rocket Launch

An example of a WBS for a Rock Concert is shown in Figure 5. We start with the Rock Concert as a project, divide it into major components such as venue, band, stage and marketing, and then further sub-divide each into smaller components until we have a Work Package that consists of a series of tasks that can be assigned to individuals.

Note that the components and work packages are associated with Nouns, and the tasks and activities are associated with Verbs. The question "What's to be done?" is answered with a noun, and "How is it to be done?" is answered with a verb. Designing a WBS for a Rocket Launch, an ERP implementation, a movie production or an election campaign is conceptually no different as it follows the same thought process.

Get together with your client, the project team and specialists who know the subject matter and start at the top with your project. With good participation and great facilitation, you will end up with a visual representation that is both meaningful and easy to follow.

Figure 5

Project Scope or Work Content View

How big is the project? What's in & What's out?
Focus on "What" before the "How"

```
                            ROCK
                           CONCERT
          ┌─────────────┬─────┴─────┬─────────────┐
        VENUE          BAND        STAGE         MRKTNG
       ┌──┴──┐      ┌───┴───┐    ┌──┴──┐      ┌───┴───┐
   RESEARCH CONTRACT SELECTION SCHEDULE A/V EQPT LIGHTS SPONSORS PROMO
                   ┌────┴────┐          ┌──┴──┐ CLIENTS TV ADS
               INTERVIEWS CONTRACT   BROCHURE           DONATIONS
                                                        TICKETS
```

Tasks and Activities Use "Verbs"

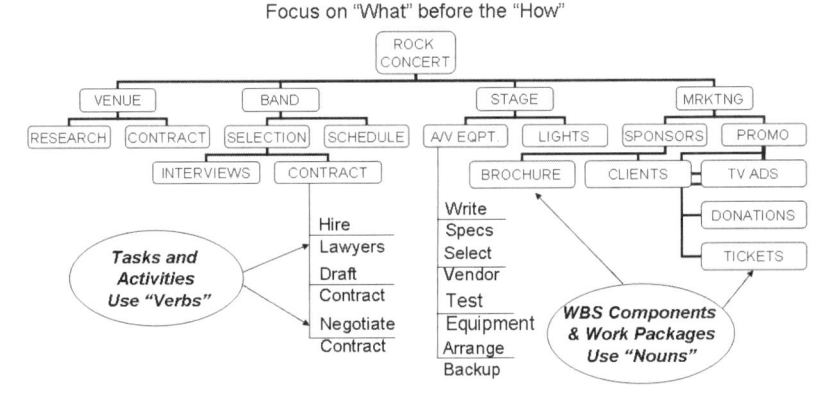

Hire Lawyers
Draft Contract
Negotiate Contract

Write Specs
Select Vendor
Test Equipment
Arrange Backup

WBS Components & Work Packages Use "Nouns"

Define the scope with Work Breakdown Structure (WBS)
Decompose into Work Packages, Deliverables & Activities

The Benefits of WBS

There is a major psychological benefit with the WBS process. It relates to the basic concept of assigning responsibility and managing people. By making people responsible for Work Packages (chunks of work) and associated deliverables, we get away from a "Task-oriented" management style. We give the team members a sense of ownership and responsibility for a set of deliverables and we stop being micro-Managers.

The end result of the WBS process is a manageable and controllable project environment that allows the Project Manager to focus on people and not on individual tasks. The WBS builds the foundation of managing all other aspects of the project. That is why successful Project Managers believe that if you don't have the WBS, then all you are working with is BS!

Organizing the Scoping Session

The Project Manager has a critical role in ensuring successful results from the scoping session. This includes organizing sessions, inviting key participants including the client and major stakeholders, facilitating the discussion, conducting iterations and reaching a consensus.

The selection of the right process for conducting the scoping sessions and its management is as important as the result in itself. The result will only be as good as the process you follow to achieve it.

Quite often, the project scoping and WBS sessions are a failure because of the following barriers to success:

- Resistance to doing the WBS

- Trying to do scope, cost and schedule development simultaneously

- Losing focus on the "Whats" and associated deliverables

- Rushing into planning with assumptions about the scope

- Expecting an automated Project Management tool to do the job

- Ignoring basic tools for analysis and problem solving such as brain-storming, facilitation and design reviews

- Lack of budget or time to do the scoping sessions resulting in pressure from management, customer & technical teams to skip the WBS

The Project Manager's challenge is to overcome those barriers and do a thorough job of scoping the project. This is where the Project Manager's skills as a facilitator are most useful. More information on facilitation skills follows in Chapter 15.

The WBS is Critical for Success

Using the Work Breakdown Structure has several benefits as it:

1. Enables a Project Manager to plan, organize, control and communicate a project

2. Provides a core foundation for all subsequent project planning

3. Establishes a systematic approach to subdividing the total project into smaller components and end products

4. Breaks up the project into conceivable and manageable pieces of work

5. Creates a common understanding of project deliverables

6. Serves as the basis for establishing a project baseline

7. Enables common, consistent and effective communication among all stakeholders

8. Serves as the primary input to scheduling and resource planning

9. Facilitates top-down project control based on bottom-up input

10. Provides the most effective vehicle to manage scope, schedule, cost and quality

Chapter Summary

Our bias is more towards jumping into action, and less towards planning and thinking. We like to get into the race without knowing where the finish line is. There is always the pressure to win the race or the contract, and the fear of losing it can cause us to lose perspective. And therein lies the source of trouble for most projects.

If the scope is not defined, understood and accepted by all parties, then the project is headed down the rat hole. Project scope has a natural tendency to inflate. This is commonly known as the dreaded "scope creep". It is a direct result of inadequate and imperfect scoping. In most cases, the root cause of scope creep is a hastily prepared requirements definition and a lack of understanding of the client's needs and expectations.

Learning Lessons

Avoid the Rat Hole – Warning Signs

1. The project does not have a Work Breakdown Structure (WBS)

2. The project has a so-called WBS that is the result of output from an automated project schedule and merely reflects the project schedule

3. The WBS is not understood and not used as a working document by the team

4. The project deliverables do not relate to the WBS

5. Project activities, instead of deliverables, are driving the project

6. The WBS exercise is bogged down by excessive iterations

Catch the "Pot of Gold" - Best Practices

1. Get a handle on the "What" before jumping into the "How"

2. Involve the client and key stakeholders in the requirements definition and project scoping discussions

3. Facilitate the WBS creation process

4. Use problem-solving skills and get consensus along the way for each iteration

5. Make WBS the foundation for planning, managing and controlling the project

6. Conduct a maximum of three iterations and you will capture 95% of the scope

06

who's doing what to whom?

Understanding the Actors and the Script

"Getting to know who is doing what to whom"

Let's open the next window and enjoy the view. This view is about Project Organization. It provides an insight into the structure and organization of the project. Project organization is quite distinct and different from the company organization.

Think of your project like directing a movie or leading an orchestra. You need to know who the players are, their roles, responsibilities and relationships. You also want to make sure that everyone has the script or the score, and is on the same page. In short, a Project Manager must have a thorough understanding of "who's doing what to whom" on the project.

The Ten Roles in a Project Organization

Let's look at the ten key roles that are critical in a project organization. They are usually designated by the following terms:

1. Management Committee or Steering Committee
2. Project Sponsor
3. Project Manager
4. Lead Designer/ Lead Engineer/ Solution Architect
5. Project Teams and Team Members
6. Client or the Customer

7. Project Stakeholders
8. Project Champion
9. End Users
10. Vendor, Sub-contractor and Consultant

Each one of these roles is inherent to a project and is performed by specific individuals who are responsible for the roles. For small and less complex projects, the role of the Project Sponsor and the Customer might be represented by the same individual. For large and complex projects, each one of the roles is uniquely defined and performed by an individual.

The very existence of multiple roles and responsibilities in a project gives rise to multiple objectives, conflicting opinions and competing priorities among the various parties. Add to that the challenges of dealing with different personalities, management styles, communication protocols, cultural differences and individual expectations - all of these form the basis of politics in Project Management.

Managing the politics of such an environment requires that the Project Manager act as a facilitator, mediator and a negotiator to ensure that the interactions among all of the players are effective and productive. Successful Project Managers leverage project politics effectively by ensuring that these roles are identified, defined and assigned to the project. Let's look at their role descriptions and what they do. The basic model for a Project Organization is shown is Figure 6.

1. Management or Steering Committee

Most organizations have a Management or Steering Committee that is made up of senior executives. The committee is responsible for establishing strategic direction and business goals. It defines and communicates management expectations and success indicators for strategic undertakings. It also provides timely resolution of strategic issues and conflicts.

The Steering Committee creates an enabling environment for driving cultural change in the organization through its people, processes and technology. It has a final say in assigning priorities among competing projects, and allocating the limited company resources to projects on hand. Finally, it is responsible for ensuring that key business objectives are met through continued reinforcement of focus, commitment and expectations.

The role of the Steering Committee is critical to the success of major projects in large organizations, especially if the scope or impact of the project cuts across functional boundaries within and outside the organization.

2. Project Sponsor

The role of the Project Sponsor is to represent the decisions of the Management or Steering Committee to the Project. The Sponsor has a vision of the project and a vested interest in its success. While bringing passion to the project, the Sponsor ensures the availability of funds for the project , and continually monitors that the project is aligned with the strategic objectives of the function, business or the organization.

The Sponsor insulates the Project Manager from high level politics in the organization, and serves as the focal point of escalation and resolution for issues outside the Project Manager's control. The Sponsor has the necessary clout and influence in the organization to drive the project across functional boundaries. Finally, the Project Sponsor is an integral part of the Project Organization, not just a "figure head".

3. Project Manager

The Project Manager role represents the single point of responsibility for the success or failure of the project. He works with all stakeholders to define project goals, objectives, critical success factors and acceptance criteria. He manages the project scope, cost, and schedule while maintaining focus on project goals and objectives. He identifies resource requirements, negotiates for priorities and resources, builds the project team and keeps it motivated towards achieving the goal. Above all, he sets expectations with the client regarding project goals and mutual responsibilities with respect to the project.

The Project Manager manages relationships and client expectations between delivery organization, clients and other stakeholders. He institutes formal communication vehicles for project planning, updates and reporting, and is always one step ahead of potential problems and project risks. He works with the client towards effective management of change through training and ongoing selling of the project. He escalates the issues that are outside his control and seeks resolution. He is loyal to his organization, the client, the product, the profession and the people in his team. Finally, the Project Manager provides leadership, a sense of purpose and motivation for the project team.

4. Lead Designer/ Design Engineer/ Solution Architect

The Lead Designer role addresses the architecture, technology and design of the proposed solution. The role may be performed by a single individual or several individuals depending on the type or complexity of the project. For a construction project, it is common to have these roles performed by different individuals and, quite often, from different organizations. For an IT organization, the Solution Architect is often the one who is responsible for the integrity of the design, and validating that the solution components will work together as expected.

The Lead Designer is responsible for designing a solution that addresses current requirements, allows for future growth and expansion, and integrates with existing infrastructure. He identifies technical risks in the design, and leads the development team in developing prototypes. He continually validates that the solution will work as planned and guides the development team towards meeting functional, performance and quality specifications based on the technology.

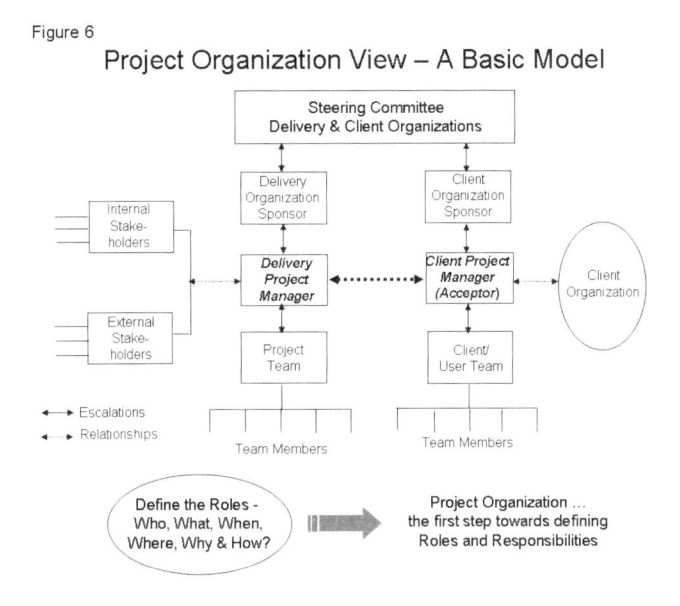

Figure 6
Project Organization View – A Basic Model

5. Stakeholder

A Stakeholder is simply anyone who has a "stake" in the outcome of the project. The term includes individuals, departments, functions or organizations that have a vested interest in the outcome of the project, and quite often, are impacted by it.

The stakeholder can be internal or external to the delivery and client's organizations. A stakeholder need not be actively involved in doing or delivering the project, or need not have an explicit decision-making role in its conduct or progress; however, he may wield significant influence on the direction of the project, and in some cases, to severely disrupt the project!

6. Client or Customer Manager

The Client Manager acts as the Project Manager's counterpart on the client side. He/She represents the client organization for decisions regarding all aspects that impact the client organization. These might include signoffs on requirements and ongoing deliverables, liaising with functional managers, coordinating internal activities, getting the buy-in at various stages of the project, managing change within the client environment and ensuring readiness for implementation.

It should be noted that the Client, in a larger context, is a stakeholder too. However, the role of the client is quite unique and critical to the project. You may have a project without a stakeholder; however, you cannot have a project without a client! Therefore, it is essential that the Client's role is recognized as a distinct entity in the Project Organization.

The absence of an identified specific individual as a Client Manager is one of the major sources of project failures. The Client Manager is the individual who makes decisions and compromises, and negotiates on behalf of the Client. Simply stated, the Project Manager and the Client Manager need each other and are dependent on each other. They work hard to develop and sustain a trusting relationship. They are "joined at the hip" and work together towards a common goal.

7. Project Champion

The role of a Project Champion is crucial for projects that result in major changes to the way an organization works including its people, policies and procedures. The Project Champion is a powerful and helpful friend of the project, and an enthusiastic spokesperson and supporter of the project.

The Champion is highly respected in the organization and has a great deal of credibility while being aloof from the politics of the project. He knows how the invisible side of the organization works, how decisions are made and "hot buttons" for the decisions. The Champion is a valuable resource to the Project Manager and provides guidance and coaching to manoeuvre the project. Enterprise type projects invariably depend on the Project Champion for their success.

8. Team Members

Projects have teams or individual team members assigned to work on various components of the project. The structure and composition of a team varies depending on the type and complexity of projects. A typical team consists of:

- *Core team members* who are usually assigned on a permanent or full time basis for the duration of the project and form the nucleus for day to day functioning of the project. The core team is passionate about the project and believes in the project. The core team members define the objectives, methodology, processes and communication norms for the project team. The core team sets the content, tone and protocol for team interaction.

- *Supporting team members* usually consist of internal functional representatives who are called upon to provide assistance to the project. Such assistance may be required from various functional specialists from Finance (for developing business justifications), Corporate Communications (for internal and external communication), Legal (for contract reviews and changes) and Purchasing (for vendor selection and contract negotiation).

- *Subject Matter Experts (SMEs)* have the knowledge and expertise in specific areas related to the project. The expertise may relate to a specific product, technology, or business process surrounding the project such as building technology, product identification, manufacturing processes, point of sale, or diagnostic imaging etc. The SMEs are called upon to provide input, validate designs and review outputs as required throughout the project.

Regardless of the type and organization structure, project teams must have a common purpose and they must believe in it to succeed. They need to be managed and motivated to achieve the project goals. They also need to have a clear understanding of each team member's role and responsibilities inside and outside the team.

9. End Users

This is where the rubber hits the road! End Users are the people who actually use the deliverables – products and services - of the project. They are the ones who will make or break the project, and determine if the project was successful. Ultimately, it is their experience and satisfaction that counts the most.

End Users are often heavily involved in project start-up activities such as defining business requirements, and participating in review, validation, testing and training activities throughout the project life cycle. It is therefore highly recommended that the Project Organization should include the User organization with assigned end users and their roles and responsibilities in the project.

10. Vendors, Sub-contractors and Consultants

This category consists of vendors, sub-contractors and external consultants associated with the project. Depending on the scope, content, role, interaction and criticality of their work, they may be directly reporting to the Project Manager as part of the project team. In such instances, they form an integral part of the project organization.

In other cases, their role may simply consist of delivering goods and services as required for the project. In any case, it should be noted that the Project Manager is responsible for managing the sub-contractor, and has ultimate responsibility for the project even if the work is sub-contracted.

Chapter Summary

Managing a project without understanding the Project Organization is like directing a play in which one doesn't know who the players are, and what they are supposed to do. Recognize these roles and know the individuals first before you start the project. As a Project Manager, you need them all to help you succeed.

A natural phenomenon that occurs with the existence of multiple roles, responsibilities and personalities is project politics. Your success depends upon how well you orchestrate their involvement, get them to cooperate effectively, and leverage the relationships that you build with them throughout the life cycle of the project. A major part of Project Management is recognizing and managing the politics of projects, and the first step is to understand the Project Organization.

Learning Lessons

Avoid the Rat Hole – Warning Signs

1. The Project doesn't have a Sponsor.

2. The Sponsor has lost interest or is not available to review the project.

3. There is confusion and finger-pointing regarding who exactly is responsible for the project. Everyone is involved, but no one is committed.

4. The stakeholders haven't been identified or involved in project decisions that might affect them.

5. The Client has not assigned an individual to the project to act as the Client Manager or Representative who is responsible to accept and sign-off the project deliverables.

6. The Client Manager is busy with day-to-day operations, and is not available for the project.

7. The client expects the Project Manager to solve his internal organizational or departmental issues as part of the project (unless that is a project objective).

8. The relationship between the Project Manager and the Client Manager is adversarial and lacks trust and cooperation. It's "us" versus "them".

9. The team members don't know their responsibilities and deliverables. There is no sense of belonging to a team.

10. The relationships among the Project Manager, Client, Vendor, Consultants, Sub-contractors, Stakeholders are not clearly defined or understood.

Catch the "Pot of Gold" - Best Practices

1. Follow the four quadrants surrounding the Project Manager role (e.g. Sponsor, Customer, Stakeholders and Team Members)

2. Question the project organization rigorously and assess validity of the project if any of the roles are missing

3. Identify the roles as they relate to your project

4. Describe the responsibilities for each role in the project

5. Identify a specific individual and assign a name for each role, and get agreement on the responsibilities

6. Publish a Project Organization chart indicating the roles and individual names

07

getting to the finish line

The Implementation Roadmap

*"If you don't know where you are going,
you'll never get there."*

We get things done when we put a stake in the ground - be it a product launch, a marketing campaign, a piece of legislation, a corporate merger or the Olympic Games. In most cases, the decision has been made (and often, the announcement too!).

The Project Manager doesn't always have the luxury of assessing if all the requirements have been defined or whether the necessary resources will be available at the right time; rather, the challenge is to get the project done by the due date while battling the unknowns and constraints. "Fast and Good Enough" is the mantra followed by many organizations to meet their project deadlines.

This is where the Implementation Roadmap comes in. It is similar to a model that an architect builds to help his clients visualize the final structure. The roadmap is a model that shows the flow of activities and events in a project from its start to finish. It is a visual representation of activities, constraints and dependencies that show how we plan to get there from here.

Preparing the Roadmap

The project roadmap consists of three stages: (1) Develop a Dependency Diagram (2) Understand the Critical Path and (3) Finalize the Project Schedule. The first stage consists of analysis, and it gives us an understanding of what and how the work should be performed. The second stage consists of synthesis, and it tells us what is driving the duration and cost of the project. The third stage helps us to "put a stake in the ground" based on available resources and other constraints, and finalize the roadmap and the schedule.

Stage 1 - Develop a Dependency Diagram

1. Start with 1 page overview of major milestones
2. List the major activities associated with each milestone
3. Understand activity relationships & dependencies
4. Develop a Network Diagram (Parallel & Series activities)

Stage 2 - Understand the Critical Path

5. Break activities into work pieces – approx. 1 week duration or less
6. Follow ground rules for estimating
7. Identify the Critical Path
8. Focus on activities on the critical path

Stage 3 - Finalize the Schedule

9. Build a schedule-constrained plan first
10. Modify the plan based on resource constraints
11. Include contingency buffer; distribute it across all project activities
12. Don't plan for overtime (It will happen anyway!)

13. Weekends, overtime etc. is similar to overdraft; use it only for contingency

14. Develop a Responsibility Assignment Matrix (also known as RACI charts)

15. Keep the schedule aggressive but achievable

Manage with Milestones

Milestones are like a series of markers or sign posts guiding you on the highway of your journey towards project completion. They tell you how far you've come, where you are in your journey and what the next marker is. They provide you with the assurance that you are headed in the right direction, and serve as intermediate goals that you can strive to accomplish. They give you and your team a continual sense of accomplishment as you progress from one goal to another. Simply stated, milestones are a series of intermediate targets, deliverables and goals that you accomplish one after another until the entire project is complete.

The markers on a highway are usually placed at strategic locations such as major cities, venues or junctions. Similarly, in a project environment, establishing milestones every 2-3 weeks is a good practice. The team members know what they have to perform and when to deliver to meet the intermediate milestones. There is greater confidence in the accuracy of planning and predictability of outcome. It is much easier to run projects by intermediate milestones spaced at 2 week intervals rather than a long 6 month period.

The use of milestones forces a sense of discipline on the project team, and when practiced with rigour and regularity, it promotes a healthy work habit. Milestones serve as the basis for "Go/ No Go" decisions along the project's journey, validate key deliverables and accomplishments, and provide a virtual picture of progress towards its goal. The dreaded last minute "surprises" are limited and addressed as they occur for each milestone, instead of waiting until it is too late.

Successful projects are managed by milestones. They serve as significant events in the progression of the project. They provide meaning and purpose to the daily work we do in the context of the overall project. Above all, they serve as an affirmation of the project's progress as planned and continually boost the confidence and morale of the team.

Dependency Diagrams – What are they?

A dependency diagram is a roadmap of how you plan to get from Point A to Point B in your project. It consists of milestones which are similar to signposts that tell you where you are in your journey, what activities you need to perform along the way and dependencies between the activities (An activity is a piece of work that consumes time).

Dependency diagrams help us to analyze different alternatives based on project constraints, and identify critical activities and the critical path. The common formats to draw the diagrams are based on two ways of representing an activity - Activity on an Arrow (AOA) and Activity in the Box (AOB). Most of the commercial Project Management software uses the AOB representation.

Preparing the Diagram – The Six Steps

Step 1.   Prepare a list of activities for each milestone

List each activity on a 3x5 index card on a sticky paper. Lay out the cards on a table and discuss the flow of activities from start to finish, and arrange them from left to right.

Step 2.   Determine the sequence of activities

Some of the activities need be performed in a sequence, while others could be done concurrently or in parallel. For example, you need to put the walls up before you paint them (there is a dependency) while you may order and receive the curtains in the meantime (can be done in parallel).

Figure 7
Project Dependency View – An Implementation Roadmap

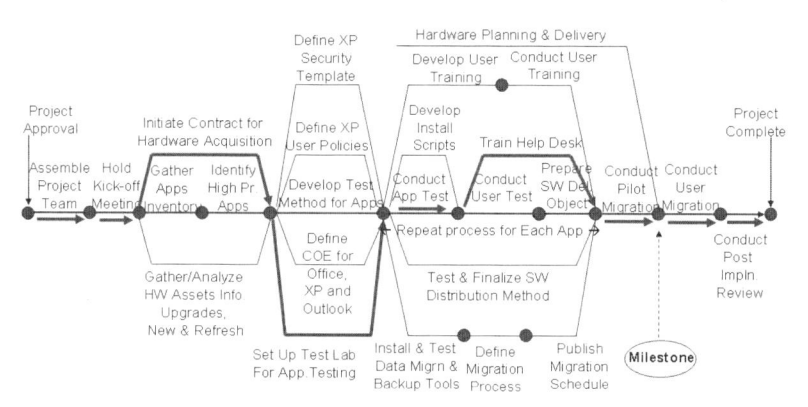

An Example of a Project Implementation Roadmap
Focus on the Critical Path, Major Milestones,
Deliverables, Dependencies and Activities

Step 3.   Develop a visual model

Focus on the flow for the first iteration and develop a visual model that shows a logical order and sequence for the activities. Leave aside the considerations regarding target date, resource constraints etc. for later iterations. Avoid the temptation to do planning, estimating and scheduling all at once.

Step 4: Estimate the duration for each activity

Make reasonable assumptions and document them. Estimate the duration of the project. It is indicated by the longest path in the dependency diagram, commonly known as the Critical Path. Now you have an idea of how long the project will take with the assumptions. You will invariably find that it exceeds the target date set by your client or the management.

Step 5: Review every activity on the critical path

Consider alternatives to expedite, accelerate, modify or move the activity with the objective of reducing the overall duration. You will end up with a new set of assumptions, dependencies and resource requirements. Perform a couple of iterations to arrive at your estimate. Aim for the optimum while making the trade-offs, not for the perfect solution.

Step 6: Present It to Management

The dependency chart makes it easy to visualize the steps in executing the project. It serves as a tool for educating the client and management in terms of understanding what is involved in the project; how it needs to be done; what is most critical; what is driving the completion date; what the alternatives and associated risks are; and where to put the resources.

It provides a bird's eye view of the project and serves as a tool for further negotiations and justification for resources. An example of a dependency diagram with an implementation roadmap for a complex Information Technology migration project is shown in Figure 7.

It's a TEAM Effort

Preparation of the roadmap is a team effort. This is what outstanding Project Managers do. They get the team involved during planning. They discuss ideas and get the client's and team members' input to arrange and rearrange the sequence of activities until a broad consensus has been reached. The process helps everyone to understand the background and rationale for the decisions. When you get them involved, you are one step closer to getting their commitment.

Let me give you an example of what happens when you run a project that is solely focused on activities. One of my clients had an elaborate project plan for a ten month project. The activities were planned for ½ day durations and several months into the future. It had about a thousand activities and close to 1,500 dependencies.

Bottom line: the Project Manager was spending all his time in updating the schedule and had no time to manage the project. A classic case of getting so wrapped up in one's underwear that one can't get out of it!

Chapter Summary

Every project must have a roadmap that articulates the flow of planned work from start to finish including major milestones, activities and the critical path. Preparation of the roadmap is a team effort requiring an exchange of ideas and healthy discussion among the team members.

The roadmap is an excellent vehicle to gain the client's confidence and management understanding of the issues and complexity of the project. The roadmap helps us to differentiate between planning and scheduling, and presents us with a bird's eye-view of the implementation process.

The process begins with understanding the "what", planning the "how" and scheduling the "when" as explained below:

- *What we do . . .*

    is driven by the project objectives and scope.

- *How it's done . . .*

    is based on the standards, conventions, technology and industry practices for the project and your business.

- *When we do it and What we commit to . . .*

    is a result of negotiations based on availability of resources, risk tolerance and achievable and realistic deadlines. This is reflected in the project baseline schedule.

Learning Lessons

Avoid the Rat Hole – Warning Signs

1. There is no distinction between planning, estimating and scheduling; the three tasks are being done concurrently.

2. There is no understanding of activities that are critical to the project.

3. There are no intermediate milestones in the project plan.

4. The scheduling exercise has become an end in itself.

5. The Client, Management and team members haven't seen the project roadmap.

Catch the "Pot of Gold" - Best Practices

1. Get the client and the project team involved in developing the roadmap

2. Present the roadmap to client and senior management

3. Identify the critical path and make sure that all members are aware of it

4. Display the roadmap with milestones, critical path and assigned resources

5. Manage the project by monitoring the critical path and milestones

08 if it's not documented, it doesn't exist!

The Discipline of Project Operations

"It ain't over until the paperwork is done."

People tend to get hung up on methodologies and then blame them for the failure of projects. My experience shows that, in most cases, the reason for failure is not the methodology itself, but the lack of discipline and commitment to follow the intent and spirit of the methodology.

What is a methodology? A methodology consists of a standardized set of Phases, Processes and Tools that are appropriate for the organization and the industry. It defines the way an organization manages its projects from initial concept to final delivery. A methodology ensures that there is a common language, terminology and discipline in the organization to successfully manage projects.

Project Phases

Project Phases define how we do business and deliver projects from beginning to end while providing a smooth transition from one phase to another. They provide a standardized and consistent way of looking at projects within an organization.

One organization might choose to divide projects into five phases such as Justification, Initiation, Definition, Implementation and Transition. Another organization might find it convenient to standardize the phases as Concept, Definition, Execution and Finish.

An engineering organization would probably look at it from a different perspective – Feasibility, Design, Prototype, Build, Test and Rollout. Choose the phase descriptions that make sense for your industry and your organization. And then, stick to them!

Project Processes

Project Processes define a standardized approach for doing work in each phase. The Project Management Institute (PMI) defines five key processes that apply to each phase – Initiating, Planning, Executing, Controlling and Closing processes. That brings us to the SIPOC cycle for each process – Who are the Suppliers to the process? What are the Inputs? What activities or transformations take place during the Process? What are the Outputs? Finally, who are the Customers that will receive the end-products of the process?

A clear understanding of each process along with its inputs and outputs is required to ensure that an organization has a consistent way of managing projects from authorization through to completion.

Project Tools

Project Tools are what you use to facilitate and often automate the work related to Project Management. They may include work such as documenting requirements, designing solutions, automating development, simulating tests, maintaining project records and facilitating communication with the project team. They include a variety of Project Management software, web-enabled applications, forms, templates etc. and they vary from one organization to another.

A common cause of the so-called "failure of a methodology" is the Project Manager's expectation of, and reliance on Project Management tools as an auto-pilot to manage the project itself. It is common to see large organizations set up a Project Management

Office (PMO), invest in new tools, train its resources, use the tools for a couple of years without genuinely adopting a methodology, blame its project failures on the tools, reorganize the shop and start the cycle all over again!

The truth is that the tools can only be used to assist, not as a substitute for Project Management. The last thing we need is a Project Manager whose only weapon is a tool. Don't be a fool with a tool!

The Project Workbook

Regardless of the methodology used, a Project Manager maintains a Project Workbook that is easily accessible for reference by team members. It consists of a series of planning documents collectively known as the Implementation or Baseline Plan, and a set of working documents required for operational and reference purposes.

The Project Workbook is the primary vehicle to ensure that the project team members have a common, consistent and clear understanding of the project and its progress. The Project Workbook requires that team members follow the discipline to put everything down in writing.

The Project Workbook is not intended to be developed on Day 1 of the project; rather, it evolves as the project progresses. It is gradually developed, revised and completed as details and information become available. The workbook for a complex project should have all of the following sections while only the relevant sections may be included for a small project.

Contents of a Project Workbook

Implementation or Baseline Plan

1. Project Charter
2. Project Organization

3. Work Breakdown Structure (WBS)
4. Major Milestones
5. Dependency Chart
6. Detailed Estimates/ Schedule
7. Deliverables/ Responsibility
8. Resource Plan
9. Financial Plan
10. Risk Management Plan
11. Project Quality Plan
12. Project Control Plan
13. Change Management Plan
14. Acceptance Plan
15. Contract Management Plan

Working Documents

16. Solution Overview
17. Work Assignments
18. Status Reports
19. Minutes of Meetings
20. Escalations & Issue Management
21. Sign-offs/ Completion Reports
22. Log of Management and Team Decisions
23. Log of Action Items
24. Terms and Conditions (T's & C's)
25. Supporting Documentation

(Requirements, Statement of Work, Proposed Solution & Architecture, Design Documents, Project Standards, Reference Manuals etc.)

Figure 8 illustrates the contents of a typical Project Workbook along with an Implementation Plan.

1. Project Charter

The Project Charter provides a high level strategic framework for the project team and the project steering committee. It establishes a common understanding of the business purpose and justification for the project. The charter clearly identifies the project sponsor, project manager, client manager, funding sources, budgetary considerations and success criteria for the project.

What it is: A statement of purpose that clearly identifies the business need, context and rationale for the project

Why you need it: To underline management's formal approval to proceed with the project and to formalize the assignment of the Project Manager

2. Project Organization

The purpose of the Project Organization document is to clearly define the roles and responsibilities of the individuals assigned to the project. The identification of a Project Manager and a Project Acceptor who are fully committed to the project is critical to the success of the project. Relationships with and responsibility of all sub-contractors, external consultants etc. should be defined in the Project Organization.

What it is: The Project Organization chart includes specific names, their roles and relationships, and it identifies the working relationships of all the individuals.

Why you need it: To ensure complete and unambiguous understanding of who is responsible for what.

3. Work Breakdown Structure

The Work Breakdown Structure (WBS) helps define the scope of the project in the form of a "family tree". It is the first step towards breaking down the project into manageable and assignable tasks, and forces the project team to define "what" before the "how". The WBS defines the scope baseline and provides the basis for measuring and reporting scope performance.

What it is: A Project Chart which defines its major components.

Why you need it: It is a proven method for identifying and controlling manageable chunks of work. It is the first step in planning the project.

4. Major Milestones

The major milestones define key events in the project life cycle and provide the means to assess whether a project is on target. Associated with each milestone are major tasks and activities which must be 100% completed for achieving the milestone. Milestones help the Project Manager differentiate a successful event from the perennial "90% complete" syndrome.

What it is: A list of significant events/accomplishments leading to project completion.

Why you need it: To serve as checkpoints in the project. Milestones are answered by a simple "Yes" or "No" and are decision points for next steps.

5. Dependency Chart

The dependency chart is the basis for project time management. The pre-requisites for developing the chart are Activity Definition, Activity Sequencing, Duration Estimating and the resolution of mandatory, discretionary and external dependencies. It is the vehicle to identify critical vs. non-critical activities and assess scheduling options during the course of the project.

What it is: A Network diagram showing dependencies and critical path for the project.

Why you need it: To show how all activities hang together, optimize resource scheduling and anticipate potential problems.

Figure 8
Project Implementation Plan – An Operational View
If it's not documented, it doesn't exist!

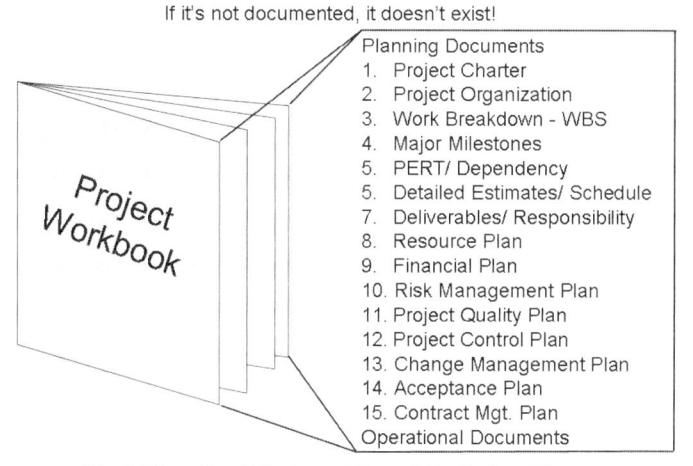

Planning Documents
1. Project Charter
2. Project Organization
3. Work Breakdown - WBS
4. Major Milestones
5. PERT/ Dependency
6. Detailed Estimates/ Schedule
7. Deliverables/ Responsibility
8. Resource Plan
9. Financial Plan
10. Risk Management Plan
11. Project Quality Plan
12. Project Control Plan
13. Change Management Plan
14. Acceptance Plan
15. Contract Mgt. Plan
Operational Documents

Project Workbook

First Plan the Work ....Then Work the Plan

6. Detailed Schedule

Developing the schedule is an iterative process based on resource availability, resource skills, and constraints due to imposed dates, key events, external suppliers and assumptions. Several techniques are used for schedule development including Project Management software, Resource Levelling and Critical Path Method. The deliverable consists of specific start & finish dates for each activity.

What it is: A comprehensive list showing planned start /completion dates, resource requirements, latest finish dates etc. for each activity. It is produced as a result of the planning process, and is considered as the Baseline schedule that is based on an agreement regarding resources, commitments and target dates.

Why you need it: This serves as the daily or weekly working document for the project team.

7. Deliverables/ Responsibility Matrix

This document outlines for each activity the individual responsible for the end product, expected deliverable from the activity, individual responsible for accepting the deliverable, completion criteria and target completion date. The intent of the document is to ensure that all individuals on the project team clearly understand their responsibilities and expected deliverables.

What it is: A document listing all the deliverables and all responsible individuals associated with the project.

Why you need it: To put the focus where it belongs - on the deliverables from each activity and people responsible for delivering it. It is a vehicle to bring visibility to the delegation of responsibility and acceptance of commitments by team members.

8. Resource Plan

The purpose of the Resource Plan is to identify the resources, skill levels and timing necessary for completing project deliverables, and to get commitment from Resource Managers. This includes any hardware and software required in the development phase. The Resource Plan is used to determine gaps in skill levels and identify training needs for the project.

What it is: A list of all resources, current vs. target skills, training plan and dates when needed on the project.

Why you need it: To gain acceptance of functional managers who provide resources.

9. Financial Plan

The Financial Plan is used for cost estimating, cost budgeting and cost control. It takes into consideration resource requirements, and provides cost estimates by milestone, cost baseline, spending plan and a cost management plan. Cost estimates are refined during the course of the project to reflect additional details. The Financial Plan is updated regularly with the project schedule to reflect cost and schedule variance, and Estimate To Complete the project (ETC).

What it is: A table or graph summarizing budgeted cost by milestone.

Why you need it: To budget project expenses, compare with actual, forecast variation and approve milestone payments.

10. Risk Management Plan

The purpose of the Risk Management Plan is to identify, as early as possible, the risk factors that are likely to affect the project. Identification of risks is followed by impact assessment, risk mitigation strategies and contingency planning. It should be noted that the impact of a risk event increases drastically as the project nears completion.

What it is: A list of known risks, probability and the amount at stake with project exposure and recommended strategies.

Why you need it: Awareness and analysis of risks makes it easier to manage the impact when they actually happen.

11. Project Quality Plan

The Quality Management Plan addresses quality attributes and measurable criteria for the project deliverables as well as the Project Management process itself. It includes operational definitions, proposed tools and techniques, expected outputs, and a list of Quality Assurance and Quality Control measures to be adopted for the project.

What it is: A clear description of quality attributes associated with end products, and the processes used to ensure them.

Why you need it: To establish common understanding of quality criteria, tools, methods and processes for the project, and to continually improve the Project Management process in the organization

12. Communication & Control Plan

The Communication and Control Plan establishes a common understanding of the process to be used for reviewing and controlling the project. It establishes the format and frequency of status reports, project reviews, follow-up procedures, and steps for escalating and resolving issues in a timely manner.

Timely identification of potential problems and accurate assessment of project status are essential for an effective Project Control Plan. The Responsibility/Accountability Matrix (RAM) Chart is one of the most effective tools used for this purpose. It is also known as the RACI chart as described in Chapter 9.

What it is: A description/chart showing how the project will be monitored and controlled.

Why you need it: Projects tend to get off track very quickly and unobtrusively. The Control Plan acts as the steering wheel to keep the project on track.

13. Change Management Plan

The Change Management Plan provides the basis for managing Change Requests. Changes to the scope of the project could be caused due to external events, errors/omissions in specifications or need to include new value-adding features.

The plan recognizes that changes are inevitable and gives a framework for evaluating their impact on the scope, time, cost and quality of the project. The evaluation will result in a decision to accept or reject the change based on a full understanding of its impact on the project.

What it is: A mutually agreed process to handle on-going changes to the project.

Why you need it: To ensure focus on the project objectives while accommodating the need to incorporate changes.

14. Acceptance Plan

The Acceptance Plan is the roadmap to ensure on-going progress of the project. It outlines the various acceptance criteria associated with each deliverable, and the process to be followed for testing, review and sign-offs for the acceptance. Scope verification is an integral part of the Acceptance Plan and it formalizes acceptance of the project scope by the stakeholders.

What it is: Description of acceptance criteria and process for each deliverable.

Why you need it: To establish a formal basis, consistent with the project objectives, for accepting or rejecting an end product.

15.   Contract Management Plan

The Contract Management Plan identifies the entire process for administering the contracts. It includes details regarding the scope of work, contractor evaluation and selection criteria, terms of the contract, administration process, acceptance criteria, and approvals (e.g. time & materials, milestone based, fixed price, cost plus etc.)

Since the contractor is responsible for a sub-project, it is expected that the contractor shall also follow the planning process outlined in steps 1-14 above. It is the Project Manager's responsibility to ensure that the contractor's plans are synchronized with the overall project plan.

What it is: Description of the work assigned to the sub-contractor, delivery plans and contract administration process. It is essentially a complete plan for the sub-project.

Why you need it: To monitor contract deliverables, assess impact on project and approve payments.

Working Documents

The Project Workbook should also consist of working documents that include:

1. Supporting and technical documentation such as Requirements Definition, Statement of Work, Design Specifications, Solution Design or Architecture, Manufacturing or Development

Specifications, Test Strategies, Test Results, Training Guides and Support and Maintenance documentation.

2. Project Control documentation such as Work Assignments, weekly Status Reports, Minutes of Meetings, Escalations to Management, Outstanding Issues Log, Sign-offs and Completion Reports.

Chapter Summary

The Schedule is not the Plan. The schedule is simply one component of the Project Implementation Plan, and it deals with the day-to-day operational aspects of managing the project. A comprehensive project plan consists of detailed documentation on all aspects of the plan from Project Charter to Project Acceptance and final signoff. The plan is revised and fine-tuned as we gain more understanding of the project and its details.

The planning job isn't done until the paperwork is completed. There must be a formal completion report at the completion of each milestone. The Project Workbook should have a collection of completion reports and signoffs. Project completion takes place on an incremental basis as intermediate milestones are achieved and signoffs are obtained. Completion must be formal, visible and documented.

Learning Lessons

Avoid the Rat Hole – Warning Signs

1. The Project Manager believes that the schedule is the Plan.

2. Project documentation does not exist, or is not current. What exists is a stack of status reports, minutes of meetings and emails.

3. Project "issues" are driving the project instead of the project plan.

4. Everyone believes that the project deadline is so tight that there is no time to plan.

5. Planning has gotten out of control and seems to be never-ending.

Catch the "Pot of Gold" - Best Practices

1. First plan the work, then work the plan

2. Facilitate the planning exercise and conduct three good iterations; you can capture 95% of the input.

3. Establish a Project Workbook and make it available to the project team

4. Have a process for revising and updating the contents of the workbook

5. Educate/Coach the sub-contractor to follow the planning process

09 who's on first?

Delegating Responsibility, Getting Commitment

"A Project gets late one day at a time"

How does a Project Manager execute and control the project? The fundamental dilemma of the Project Manager is that of Responsibility versus Authority. While a Project Manager has 100% responsibility for the success or failure of the project, the authority is quite limited, and often minimal, in terms of direct control over resources, client's needs, changing circumstances and unexpected events.

The Project Manager's authority, while not always explicit, is implicit in the role that is assigned. It is role-based and it follows from the expectation that the Project Manager will do everything possible as a professional, to manage client's expectations and achieve the project outcome.

As such, you have as much authority as you think you have. If you think you have none, then you have none. If you think you have it, then you have it. What you need are the skills and maturity to exercise that authority with tact, focus, sensitivity, integrity and professionalism.

The Project Manager always has the authority to delegate work and to follow up on assignments. It includes the authority to sell the project at all times, and to identify and act upon potential risks. It extends to accepting or rejecting change requests, obtaining sign offs, approving milestone payments and escalating issues.

The Project Manager has the authority to wave the red flag for help regarding issues that are outside his control. This authority goes with the job and the role, and it has to be exercised in order to be understood.

Authority, Responsibility & Commitment

Successful Project Managers clearly understand how to exercise authority, delegate responsibility and obtain commitments.

1. **Authority is exercised**

    The Project Manager is aware of his/her own implicit authority, and knows how to exercise it with respect to the client, team, management, supplier and all other stakeholders. Part of the Project Manager's authority flows from the Project Charter and it is explicit. Part of the authority is inherent and is derived from the Project Manager's role.

2. **Responsibilities are delegated**

    The Project Manager knows how to delegate responsibility while acknowledging that it can be delegated, but not abdicated. Delegation is not about splitting, sharing or transferring responsibility. It is about being 100% accountable for actions, decisions and results of the work that have been delegated.

3. **Commitments are accepted**

    The person accepting commitments must clearly understand what the deliverables are, and who will be accepting them. For delegation to be effective, there must be a positive acknowledgement of commitment by the acceptor. Deliverables provide the linkage between the delegation of responsibility and the acceptance of commitment.

The Politics of Projects

The subject of authority, responsibility and commitments is closely interwoven with organizational politics. Organizations suffer from, and quite often thrive on politics that include conflicting objectives, competing goals and confusing priorities resulting in many opinions, disagreements, lack of commitment, personal biases and employee dissatisfaction. That's the nature of organizations.

A Project exists to serve a business need in an organization. As such, it is subject to assumptions, constraints and expectations of various functions, departments and individuals in the organization. A Project Manager has to recognize and understand the elements of politics, and be able to manoeuvre the project toward a successful outcome. Politics are simply unavoidable in Project Management.

Consequently, it is the Project Manager's job to motivate all of the players to move in the same direction with respect to the project. The Project Manager, therefore, has no choice but to be an active player in the politics of projects and Project Management. There is a difference, however, in the way an outstanding Project Manager views and practices it.

Politics need not have a negative connotation for a Project Manager. One can engage in playing the politics of projects without necessarily viewing it as a dirty game. In a positive sense, one can think of politics as the ability to influence events and people to steer the project towards its objectives and achieve the intended outcome.

That is what one does in order to get someone's buy-in, negotiate for resources, manage change requests, handle team conflicts, champion the cause, seek budget approvals, and so on. The art of influencing starts with effective communication skills.

Delegating Responsibility

The RACI Chart – Tool for Effective Delegation & Communication

Delegating work to team members and getting their enthusiastic commitment is a key function of Project Management. One of the tools for achieving effective delegation and related communication is a chart which derives its name RACI from four basic roles associated with Responsibility, Approval, Consultation and Information. The RACI chart is a powerful tool for clearly defining and delegating responsibilities.

As illustrated in Figure 9, it is simply a matrix that consists of a list of deliverables, and a list of individuals along with their roles on the project. For each deliverable, you fill in the matrix by identifying:

- The individual responsible for delivering it (R)

- The individual who is responsible for approving or accepting the completed deliverable (A)

- The individual(s) who must be consulted, based on their knowledge and expertise relative to the deliverable(C)

- The individuals who need to be kept informed of any significant steps or events along the way (I).

The completed matrix is called the RACI chart, which is also known as the Responsibility Assignment Matrix (RAM) chart.

Guidelines for preparing and using the RACI chart

1. Have a list of work packages and deliverables ready for discussion (These follow from the Work Breakdown Structure for the project)

2. Get the team involved and discuss the individuals and responsibilities to be assigned to the R,A,C and I roles

3. Fill in the chart, working with each work package or deliverable at a time

4. Include additional information regarding Target Date and Budget for each item

5. Provide an initial draft for review by the participants, conduct 1-2 iterations to produce the final version

Figure 9

Responsibility and Accountability View
Manage Project Deliverables with the "RACI" Chart

Work Package/ Deliverable	Project Manager	Client Manager	Business Analyst	Technical Architect	Developer No. 1	Network Analyst	End User Rep.	Target Date	Cost
Work Pkg # 1									
- Deliverable 1		A	R		I		C	03/06	$
- Deliverable N		I	C	A		R		03/31	$
Work Pkg # 2									
- Deliverable 1	C		I		R		A	04/10	$
- Deliverable N			A	C		I	R	07/15	$
Work Pkg # N									
- Deliverable 1	R	A	C	I				06/01	$
- Deliverable N		R	A	I	C			06/14	$

R : Responsible for the Deliverable   A : Accepts/ Approves the deliverable
C : Must be Consulted   I : Needs to be Informed

Benefits of the RACI Chart

The final RACI chart reflects the consensus of the team. It eliminates ambiguities with respect to responsibilities. It helps to develop cooperation among the team players who must work together to deliver a product. It minimizes the need for redundant communication and it makes everyone's role and commitments visible. It secures the team's participation in the decision-making process which ultimately builds individual commitment.

Project Monitoring & Control

Project Monitoring and Control has two objectives: Monitoring helps the Project Manager to focus on future plans and adjustments in relation to the project goals; Controlling provides performance-based measures and indicators to assess how well the project is progressing. Monitor the following to assess how well the project is progressing in relation to the project plan:

What Should You Monitor?

1. Number of Milestones completed . . . *Not* Number of Activities

2. Number of Deliverables completed . . . *Not* Volume of documentation

3. Number of Signoffs obtained . . . *Not* Number of issues resolved

4. Progress along the Critical Path . . . *Not* Detailed Schedule

5. Productivity of the Team . . . *Not* Overtime Hours

6. Team Morale & Motivation . . . *Not* Team Politics

7. Earned Value . . . *Not* Work already done

8. Estimate to Complete (Effort) . . . *Not* % work completed

9. Estimate to Complete ($) . . . *Not* % of budget spent

10. Impact of Change Requests . . . *Not* Number of Change Requests

11. Customer Relationship . . . *Not* Reporting Tools

12. Project Risks . . . *Not* Project Assumptions

13. Management of Change . . . *Not* Resistance to Change

14. User Participation & Enthusiasm . . . *Not* number of meetings

15. Project Outcome re Business Needs . . . *Not* Project Output

Project Performance Indicators

Track the following project performance indicators and look for warning signals:

- Project high risk areas
- Overview of project progress
- Project Cost, Earned Value, Estimate to Complete
- Status of scheduled activities
- Potential problems/ Outstanding issues
- Status of action items
- Overall project outlook

Part of monitoring consists of identifying potential problems before they occur, and taking appropriate actions. Some actions may fall within the sphere of the authority and control of the Project Manager, while there might be some that fall outside the Project Manager's control.

An organizational change, the sudden resignation of a key resource, changes in the customer's environment, employee strikes, unexpected delays in delivery etc. are examples of problems that are outside the control of the Project Manager.

Your responsibility, when faced with these situations, is to alert the Project Sponsor of their impact on the project, escalate the issues for resolution, and provide alternatives and recommendations to management. Failure to do this can result in unpleasant surprises and sink a project into a rat hole.

Projects Get Late ….. One Day at a Time

How often do you find that someone drops a bombshell in a meeting by announcing something like this when it is least expected:

"We are going to be late by two months", or

"The design doesn't work because our assumptions were wrong", or

"The costs have gone up by 50%".

None of these things happened on a specific day at a specific time. Rather, the issues and problems had been festering for a long time. Either we have tried to ignore them, or suppress them in the hope that they will go away. They seldom do, and they come back to bite us at the worst possible times. That's why it is important to continually monitor and act on the resolution of potential problems.

Remember, projects get late one day at a time!

Micro-management Won't Get You There!

Micro-management - getting lost in the woods and losing sight of the forest – is the number one killer of projects. It gives the false impression of lots of activity, and undermines productivity. It deprives people of a sense of accomplishment and acts as a de-motivator.

The practice of micro-managing is built on the belief that people don't understand how to do their work, and they need to be supervised constantly. It undermines the value of an individual's contribution, destroys creativity, thwarts initiative and dampens enthusiasm. People are motivated and challenged when you make them responsible for a chunk of work and the associated end results.

The outstanding Project Manager guides and coaches the team members towards completing their assignments rather than breathing down their necks. Avoid micro-managing: give the team the big picture and ask for their input. Don't tell them how to do their job. Rather, ask them for their ideas, expertise and input to plans. Cultivate a sense of ownership among the team members.

The anti-dote to micro management is to focus on milestones, agree on the deliverables and let the team members do their job knowing that the Project Manager is there when needed.

Chapter Summary

The Project Manager has the implicit authority to get the work done and drive the project towards a successful outcome. The Project Manager shoulders 100% responsibility for the project. The Project Manager gets work done through delegation, communication and control. Responsibilities are delegated. Commitments are accepted. What ties them together is a package of deliverables and results. The RACI Chart is a powerful tool for achieving delegation and ensuring commitment.

The Project Manager is responsible for ongoing monitoring and controlling of the project using appropriate measures and performance indicators. The Project Manager stays away from micro-management. Rather, he strives to develop the skills and competencies of team members and encourages them to fully contribute to the project. Organizational politics is a fact of life. Experienced Project Managers practice it in a positive sense, by building relationships and exercising influencing skills.

Learning Lessons

Avoid the Rat Hole – Warning Signs

1. Team members don't know who is responsible for doing what on the project

2. The Project Manager's authority is in doubt, not respected or not accepted

3. Management's and the Client's commitment to the project is "Luke warm"

4. The Project Manager avoids meeting with the Client and other stakeholders

5. The Project Manager doesn't have the confidence that he/she can get the project done

6. There are frequent last minute slippages or surprises regarding project schedule or cost

7. The project team is spending more time on managing changes as opposed to managing the project

Catch the "Pot of Gold" - Best Practices

1. Develop your network of contacts in the organization

2. Monitor the right indicators for the project

3. Develop, distribute and display RACI charts

4. Continually validate team member's understanding of responsibilities and commitments

5. Conduct de-briefing sessions throughout the project (e.g. end of phase, significant milestone etc.)

10 uncertainty
- the only certainty

Project without Risks is a Fantasy!

*"What we anticipate seldom occurs;
what we least expected generally happens."*
– Benjamin Disraeli

The concept of risk is inherent to a project. A risk is an event that may or may not occur in the future. It usually results in a negative, or sometimes, in a positive impact on the scope, schedule, quality or budget of the project when it occurs. Risks are not static. They change in terms of characteristics, magnitude and impact as the project progresses from start to finish.

During the initial stages of a project, the risk is high. If the risk event occurs, during this period, its impact is low. The high risk stems from the fact that we don't have adequate details about the project. The impact is low since the project has just started, there is not a whole lot of investment made in the project, and there is adequate time to recover from the risk event, if it happens.

The risk-impact scenario is quite different in the later stages as we approach project completion. We know a whole lot about the project, and therefore, the probability of the risk event is low. However, if it does happen, then the impact can be very high. The Project Manager should always be scanning the horizon for major risks that might impact the project.

Risks and Assumptions

The Project Manager needs to clearly differentiate between Risks, Assumptions, Issues and Changes.

Risk is a possible future event. We need to plan for it and be prepared to execute the plan if the risk occurs. The planning requires a clear understanding of roles and responsibilities so that the team can respond quickly, efficiently and effectively. A risk, once accepted, serves no more as a reason for not doing the project; rather, it is a conscious decision to go ahead with a plan and make preparations to manage the risk.

There is often the tendency to cover all risks with assumptions. For example, let's say that we are constructing a building. The Project Manager develops the project plan with the assumption that it won't rain. When it actually rains and the project is delayed because of it, the unacceptable response is, "It's not my fault, check the assumption."

What happened in this case? The Project Manager took a risk and turned it into an assumption that was unrealistic. An assumption usually serves as an escape clause, an excuse or a prop for the Project Manager, and it gives the mistaken impression that it will provide some kind of protection in case of non-performance. Firstly, no one reads the assumptions, and secondly, assumptions are seldom contractually binding.

An assumption must be realistic, verifiable, challenged and validated for it to be reasonable. Minimize the assumptions that you make for your project plans. If you have to make any assumptions, ensure that they are realistic before starting the project. Modify the project plans if the assumption changes, and keep the client informed.

Remember, you're on the hook for delivering the project even if there is a laundry list of assumptions. The best way to treat assumptions is to turn them around into project requirements and build the project plans accordingly. An assumption doesn't change the situation! We make assumptions, and we plan for risks.

Issues and Changes

Issues relate to the present. We are faced with situations that are happening now. They need to be recognized, prioritized and resolved. Seasoned Project Managers develop and obtain the client's agreement on a process for analyzing, escalating and resolving issues. When issues come up, as they often will, then you can follow the process.

Changes relate to deviation from previously agreed constraints regarding scope, cost, time and quality. They are a fact of life. They arise from many causes: Language isn't perfect, the client doesn't know exactly what he wants, the technology is evolving or untested, the market has changed, the funding is reduced, and so on. No amount of "freezing" the specifications is going to eliminate the need for changes. Expect a change and be prepared to deal with it positively.

Managing Change Requests

The ability to manage Change Requests is the key differentiator for successful projects. They need to be addressed through a formalized Change Control process. The process consists of recording the change request, evaluating it, determining its impact on the project, and obtaining formal approvals to implement the change.

Define the process first and let everyone know how it is to be followed for change requests. The details of the process may vary depending upon the type of projects. However, a Change Control process is absolutely critical in a Project Management environment. If it is neglected, you will certainly have a situation where you are managing mostly the changes but not the project.

Sources of Risk

There are many sources of risks in the project:

- Use of new or untested technology

- Change in the company's strategic direction or business policy

- Complexity of design, architecture and the solution

- Level of cooperation among the client and delivery organizations

- Cooperation and readiness of stakeholders to support the project

- Management of change relative to people, process and technology

- Vague or evolving requirements

- Changing Scope

Identifying Risks - Using the TIMO Approach

Identifying genuine and relevant risks at any stage of the project requires a disciplined approach for discussion of ideas, analysis and synthesis of data. This is accomplished through good facilitation, usually provided by the Project Manager.

One way to achieve this is by analyzing project risks and grouping them as into four categories (e.g. Technology, Implementation, Management and Organizational – TIMO) and identifying the top two or three risks for each category that could jeopardize the outcome of the project. This approach is illustrated in Figure 10.

Figure 10
Project Risk and Uncertainty View

The Universe is Hostile to the Success of Your Projects!

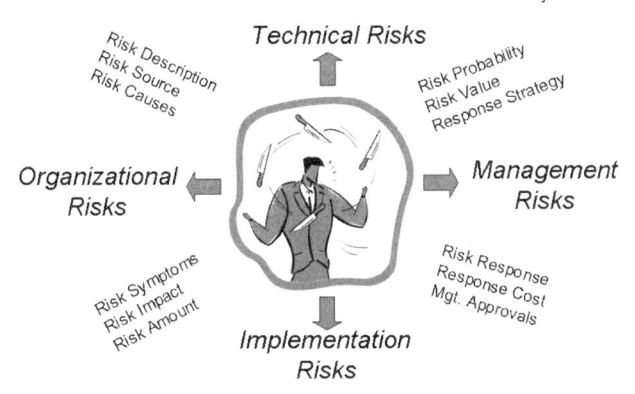

Technical Risks

Risk Description
Risk Source
Risk Causes

Risk Probability
Risk Value
Response Strategy

Organizational Risks

Management Risks

Risk Symptoms
Risk Impact
Risk Amount

Risk Response
Response Cost
Mgt. Approvals

Implementation Risks

Identify, Evaluate and Manage Project Risks

1. Technology Risks

There are many sources of risks related to technology. These include the use of new or unproved technology, timely availability of technology, its integration with other solution components, supplier's capability to deliver the technology, and the time required to become familiar with it.

2. Implementation Risks

The primary sources of risk related to implementation are lack of skilled resources, scheduling conflicts, changes to project priorities, readiness for implementation, management of organizational and process change, and the transition to operations following project implementation.

3. Management Risks

Management risks can generally be attributed to ambiguous requirements, differences in expectations, lack of common understanding about project objectives and the absence of buy-in from functional managers and stakeholders. A major source of management risks is the lack of commitment and priority for the project by those who are most impacted by it.

4. *Organizational Risks*

The factors that contribute to organizational risks are: resistance to change, lack of enthusiasm, low morale among the team members, adversarial relationship between the Project Manager and the Client Manager, scepticism among union representatives, and a general absence of trust among the project players. Quite often, this is a reflection of the culture of the organization.

The Project Manager's failure to recognize, identify and manage these risks, in both the delivery and client organizations, can defeat the best laid plans for the project and result in severe consequences for the project.

Risk Mitigation & Contingency Planning

An assessment of risks requires a culture of openness where the team members are encouraged to discuss them. A project environment where people feel threatened to discuss the risks and consequences will generally end up in failure (Refer to NASA story). There are four strategies for mitigating risks – You can decide to accept the risk, avoid the risk, reduce the risk or transfer the risk.

If the strategy calls for accepting the risk, then you need to develop a contingency plan and execute it, should the risk occur. If you wish to avoid the risk, then you'd better eliminate the risk by removing its cause. If you choose to reduce the risk, then your options consist of reducing the probability of its occurrence or its monetary impact on the project. Finally, with the transfer strategy, you are transferring all or part of the risk to a third party.

There are costs and consequences associated with each strategy resulting in what is known as the Expected Monetary Value (EMV) which is used as a guideline for decision making. The Project Manager's responsibility is to analyze the strategies and recommend the appropriate one to management for approval.

The ultimate decision to accept a specific risk and strategy rests with the management, while the responsibility to develop the plan and manage the risk rests with the Project Manager. The key is to ensure that one has an up to date risk management plan regardless of the strategy.

Managing Risks – A Simple Approach

1. Risk Description: What is the risk?

2. Risk Source: Where and When is it likely to occur?

3. Risk Causes: What are the likely causes?

4. Risk Symptoms: What are the triggers?

5. Risk Impact: Critical, High, Medium or Low

6. Risk Amount: Effect on Project $ if no action is taken

7. Risk Probability: Probability of risk occurring if no action is taken

8. Risk Value: Estimated $ value (Risk Amount X Probability)

9. Risk Response Strategy   Alternatives & Recommended Strategy (Avoidance, Reduction, Transfer or Accept)

10.	Risk Response:	Actions to implement Response Strategy
11.	Response Cost:	Estimated cost to execute the Risk response
12.	Mgt. Approvals:	Agreement on Strategy, Response & Cost

Regardless of the response strategy selected for the risk, the Project Manager is responsible for developing the response plan and managing project risks.

Symptoms of Potential Risk

1. No one knows who is in charge of the project
2. Project Organization is not clearly understood
3. Business benefits and objectives are questionable
4. There is no identified sponsor for the project
5. There are no identified stakeholders for the project
6. The project solution is not reviewed and validated by the team
7. Project activities are not detailed within a two week duration
8. There is no change control process; if it's there, it doesn't work
9. There is no planning regarding the management of change in the organization
10. Management wants to hear only the good news – no real reporting
11. Project Documentation/Standards are not consistently used by the team

12. The needed level of experience and confidence in the project is lacking

Chapter Summary

Risk Management deals with today's decisions regarding future risk events in the life of a project. The risk events may originate from a number of issues and sources related to Technology, Implementation, Management and Organization (TIMO). The Project Manager is responsible for identifying and evaluating the risks, and recommending to management appropriate strategies to mitigate the risks.

The decision to take the risk rests with senior management. However, the responsibility of the Project Manager is to maintain an up to date risk management plan, and be ready to execute it if and when the risk event occurs. Risk is managed throughout the project life cycle. When it comes to managing risks, the Project Manager "thinks like a pessimist, and acts like an optimist".

Learning Lessons

Avoid the Rat Hole – Warning Signs

1. Management does not want to hear about risks

2. The Project Manager doesn't know what the top three risks are and doesn't have a "Ready to Execute" plan if the risk event occurs

3. Project Budget does not include funding for the approved risk strategies

4. People are confusing project constraints with project risks

5. You are managing issues most of the time, not the project

Catch the "Pot of Gold" - Best Practices

1. Identify the top three risks related to TIMO - Technology, Implementation, Management & Organizational considerations for the project

2. Have an up to date list of the top three risks that may jeopardize the project over the short term (four weeks) and long term (three months)

3. Prepare a Risk Management Plan based on your mitigation strategy

4. Have a "Ready to Execute" Risk Management plan

5. Include risk funding as part of the project

6. Get the Risk Management plan approved by the Senior Management

7. Make risk review a permanent agenda item in your project review meetings

11 the cost is the cost is the cost

The Mystery of "Runaway" Projects

"You can't control what you can't measure."

Cost management is your financial window into the world of Project Management. It addresses what it will take financially to get the project done, and how you get there. It deals with the following areas for cost estimating, budgeting, monitoring and ongoing financial performance of the project:

- Preparation of a cost estimate
- Preparation of a baseline budget
- Developing cumulative budget and actual costs
- Determining the earned value of work performed
- Analyzing cost performance
- Forecasting project cost at completion
- Controlling project costs
- Managing cash flow

Cost Estimating

There is a vast difference between the theory and practice of cost estimating. The theory provides a step by step process for coming up with cost estimates using one or more of the following approaches:

1. Professional or Expert judgement

2. Historical approach: Top Down or "Analogous" costing based on actual cost of a similar project

3. Standards approach or Parametric modeling: Based on project parameters and mathematical models such as cost per unit

4. Bottom Up Estimate: Developed from a detailed estimate of each work package. WBS is the source

5. Factored: Remaining costs are percentages of main equipment or phase costs

In practice, however, cost estimating is highly influenced by what the client is willing to pay, or what the vendor wishes to charge to win the business at a profit or a loss that is acceptable. This is a market reality. The interplay between project cost and final pricing gets quite confusing from the Project Manager's perspective.

The Cost is the Cost is the Cost

The project cost is relatively constant in relation to the scope of a project, assuming no drastic variation in labour rates, and the cost of equipment and materials. The bottom line cost can be improved by looking into various alternatives. However, once an agreement is reached, the cost doesn't change, and it cannot be renegotiated unless the parameters for scope, schedule and quality also change.

The price, however, is determined by market pressures, competition and management's expectation of acceptable profit or loss. The price is what the client pays for the value received from the project. It can be negotiated, and it is not necessarily fixed in relation to the scope of the project. The Project Manager is responsible for managing the cost, not the price.

The EFGs of Cost Estimating

There are three types of cost estimates commonly known as:

- Order of Magnitude or "Elevator Talk" estimate (E)
- Budgetary or "Financial" estimate (F)
- Definitive or "Good/ Granular" estimate (G)

1. "Elevator Talk" or Order of Magnitude Estimate

The Order of Magnitude estimate is often based on comparison with other projects that are similar in size, scope, complexity and use of technology. In the absence of examples for comparison, one may resort to an educated guess. It is ultimately an approximation made without detailed information, evidence or data. It is used during the formative stages of an expenditure program for a high level evaluation of the project. It is known in the industry by various terms such as preliminary, conceptual, initial, ball park and SWAG estimate. The accuracy of the Order of Magnitude estimate is in the -30% to +50% range.

2. "Financial" or Budgetary Estimate

The Budgetary estimate is established on the basis of quantitative information derived from specifications, a mixture of firm and unit prices for labour, material and equipment. The financial estimate is sometimes referred to as approximate, control, design development or semi-detailed estimate. This type of estimate is used to allocate money into an organization's budget for one to two years into the future. The accuracy of the financial estimate is typically in the -15% to +30% range.

3. **"Good" or Definitive Estimate**

This is the final estimate that is actually reflected in the working schedule and costs. The Definitive Estimate is prepared from well defined data, drawings and specifications. It is used for bid proposals, pre-tender estimates, bid evaluations, contract changes and claims evaluation. It deals with estimating the final project costs. The accuracy of the Definitive estimate is typically in the -5% to +15% range.

Beware of the "Ball Park"

Imagine being asked to provide a fixed cost estimate for a project which is still in the conceptual stage, where the specs can't be frozen, the requirements are continually evolving and the technology is unknown or unproven. Nevertheless, the clients and Project Managers engage themselves in a ritual of dance surrounding the notion of "Ball Park" estimate based on an idea.

The Project Manager is eager to impress the audience with a quick response based on a wild guess, while the management and the client assume that the numbers are highly padded and can be shaved. The process of negotiation has already started without the slightest idea about the size, scope and complexity of the project.

The "ball park" estimate somehow gets engraved in stone as the final approved budget! Talk about committing a conscious act of Hara-Keri! How does one get around this situation? Experienced Project Managers use the principle of "Incremental Planning" to set the cost budget and manage expectations.

Cost Budgeting

The purpose of cost budgeting is to establish a cost baseline. It helps us to express the estimate in a meaningful way that enables the Project Manager to perform cost monitoring, cost control and cash flow forecasting. It establishes a common frame of reference for the purpose of sharing financial information and monitoring project performance. Figure 11 lists the major steps involved in Cost Planning, Estimating, Budgeting and Control.

Project budgeting is a three step process:

1. Identify the work packages in the project WBS. The packages are associated with costs and specific responsibilities and they serve as "control accounts" for cost budgeting.
2. Develop and allocate the cost estimate for each work package in the project WBS.
3. Distribute the budget for each work package over the duration of the work package.

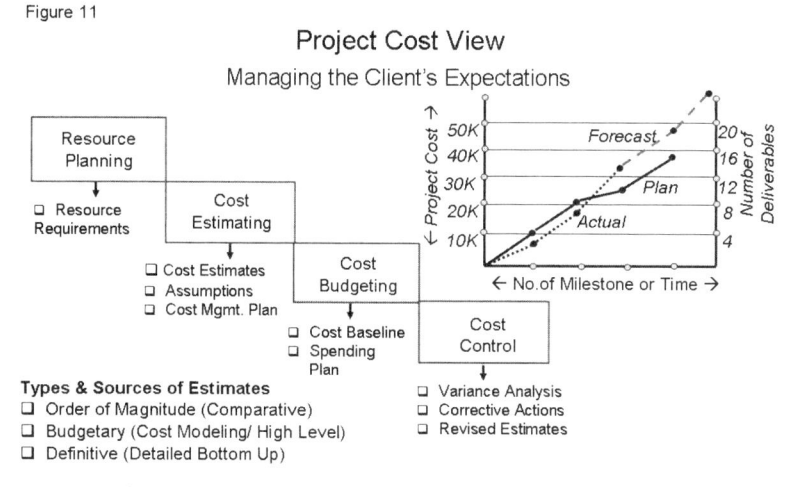

Figure 11

Project Cost View
Managing the Client's Expectations

- Resource Planning
  - Resource Requirements
- Cost Estimating
  - Cost Estimates
  - Assumptions
  - Cost Mgmt. Plan
- Cost Budgeting
  - Cost Baseline
  - Spending Plan
- Cost Control
  - Variance Analysis
  - Corrective Actions
  - Revised Estimates

Types & Sources of Estimates
- Order of Magnitude (Comparative)
- Budgetary (Cost Modeling/ High Level)
- Definitive (Detailed Bottom Up)

Focus on "Earned Value", "Actual to date", "Cost Variance", "Schedule Variance", "Deliverables" and "Estimate to Complete"

There are two other factors that influence budgeting. They are: Contingency Reserve and Risk Management budget.

Contingency Reserve is a budgetary item that reflects management's decision to allow for additional costs based on prior experience, organizational practices and practical considerations such as vacation time, sick time and work practices.

It is based on the understanding that the costs will be incurred somewhere or sometime during the project, although its timing cannot be clearly identified. The distribution of contingency reserve across the project is determined by the management. Contingency Reserves are meant to be used.

Risk Management budget is based on management's decision regarding the risk strategies approved for the project. It makes provision for funds to implement the risk responses, should the risk events occur. As such, the Risk Management budget must be included in the project budget, but it may only be used if the risk event occurs.

Life Cycle Costing: This is used for large scale projects that have a life span of several years. Its purpose is to assess the project's financial viability based on all costs including capital costs, operational costs and dismantling or salvaging costs. It looks into the delivery, operation and disposal of the project's end products to get an overall financial picture, and applies present value analysis to get at the real costs.

The concept of Life Cycle Costing is highly useful for evaluating alternatives and estimating rate of return based on project investment (ROI). Some examples of Life Cycle Costing include building an oil refinery, constructing a nuclear power generation station or erecting a steel manufacturing plant.

The Principle of Incremental Planning

The shorter the time frame, the better the estimate! Incremental Planning is based on the principle that our accuracy in forecasting the future is much better with manageable time horizons for planning. We are much better at estimating and forecasting costs, for example, over the next 30-45 days than over the next 12 months.

It also takes into consideration the fact that there is inherent tension between our ability to influence cost and the degree of information available at any one point of time. The reality is that project costs are highly influenced in the early stages of the project when information exists only at a conceptual level, and is not detailed enough to make accurate estimates.

Incremental planning helps us to continually look at forecasting from two perspectives:

1. Short term forecast with a high degree of certainty and accuracy, usually in the -5% to +15% range. This applies to work that is planned over the next 30-45 days.

2. Long term forecasts with a lower level of accuracy in the -15% to +30% range. This applies to work that is planned to be delivered beyond the 45 days timeframe.

The project forecast is constructed using both the short term and long term forecasts, and continually refined as work progresses from one phase to another. With the completion of each project phase, there is added clarity and more information for the task ahead. The forecasting accuracy improves as the project progresses. This is the way to manage the client's expectations: Provide reliable estimates based on available information and estimating accuracy, and refine it as the project progresses.

Calendar Time Vs. Effort Relationship

The estimating exercise is often flawed due to the lack of clarity regarding time, effort and productivity. Time refers to the available calendar days while effort refers to the actual days and productive work. There are 365 calendar days in a year while the number of actual working days is around 220 once we allow for weekends, statutory holidays, vacations, training and sick leave.

In other words, we can expect one full time employee (FTE) to contribute the equivalent of 220 workdays of effort over one year assuming 100% productivity. There are several factors, however, that come into play and they reduce the productivity of the individual. The major ones include employee experience, motivation, job related skills, need for rework, travel time, project meetings, administrative work and project communication including email and voice mail. The larger the size of the team, the more the time spent on team interaction and communication.

The end result is that the actual average productivity under the best of circumstances is closer to 200 workdays of effort. That's only 1,600 work hours based on 8 hours per day! How does this affect costing considerations? If we are looking at a one year project, are we talking about 365 days of effort, 220 days of effort or 200 days of effort? The answer in each case is significantly different as you will need 1.8 FTE, 1.5 FTE or 1 FTE depending on your costing assumptions.

That's a variation of 80% in estimating project resources! When you are dealing with larger teams and longer timeframes, the impact can be devastating. For small teams and shorter timeframes (up to four weeks) it may be possible to achieve 100% productivity. However, this doesn't hold true for large projects and longer timeframes.

Cost Performance – Basic Terminology

For the Project Manager, the key terminology for cost management consists of Budgeted Cost, Actual Cost, Variance, Earned Value and Estimate to Complete.

Budgeted cost is obtained as a result of the baseline. *Actual cost* is incurred as resources are expended on the project. *Variance* is the difference between the budgeted and actual costs. The variance can be measured in several ways in relation to the project schedule, set of deliverables or milestones completed. Estimate to Complete *(ETC)* looks ahead from what has been accomplished to date, and projects how much more will be required to complete the remaining work.

Earned value is the budgeted cost of the work actually performed. It is determined by collecting data on each work package and estimating the percentage of work completed. The percentages are then converted to a dollar amount or work hours based on the budgeted cost. Earned value gives us an overall perspective of project performance in relation to scope, cost and schedule.

The ABCs of Cost Management

Outstanding Project Managers understand the following terminology and manage their project costs with six basic measures. They are TBC, CBC, CAC, CEV, ETC and VAR.

TBC (Total Budgeted Cost) is the sum total of the baseline budget for the project

CBC (Cumulative Budgeted Cost) is the cumulative budget for work packages, project deliverables or milestones

CAC (Cumulative Actual Cost) is the cumulative actual cost based on work packages delivered or milestones completed, and accepted by the client

CEV (Cumulative Earned Value) is the cumulative value of work delivered on the project and it serves as a reliable indicator of how well the overall project is doing.

ETC (Estimate to Complete) is the sum total of dollars or work hours required to complete the outstanding project work

VAR (Variance) is the difference between budgeted and actual cost

Taken together, these measures go way beyond just tracking project expenditures. They constitute the equivalent of a "score card" for the financial health of the project. They help us to understand how we got to where we are, and prompt us to focus on future commitments. They can be effectively used to educate the project team, create cost awareness and manage the client's expectations. The measures serve as a financial compass for the project without which the project is like a ship that is lost on the high seas.

Chapter Summary

Projects consume resources that cost money. Project costs have to be planned, estimated and budgeted for the duration of the project, and continually monitored. The concept of "Incremental Planning" can help the Project Manager to set the client's expectations with different types of estimating techniques.

Projects that are longer than 3-4 months in duration are significantly impacted by factors associated with accuracy of forecasting, available working days and team productivity. Cost Management is most effective when it is used in conjunction with the six primary measures related to budgeted and actual cost, earned value and estimate to complete.

Learning Lessons

Avoid the Rat Hole – Warning Signs

1. There is no distinction between "Order of Magnitude", Budgetary and Firm cost estimates

2. Project costs do not include all of the cost elements and funding for risk management and management reserves

3. Management expectation of project cost is not aligned with the estimate to complete the project

4. There are no formal and documented management and client approvals for cost overruns and escalating costs

5. There is pressure from outside the project team to undermine, understate or hide the true project costs

Catch the "Pot of Gold" - Best Practices

1. Develop costs based on estimated workdays and productivity

2. Include budget for risk management depending on the risk strategy

3. Monitor the budgeted cost, actual cost and variance by deliverables and milestones

4. Focus on earned value and estimate to complete at every major milestone

5. Continually manage the client's expectations by reporting an up to date and accurate picture of all costs

12

quality is what the client experiences

The Product and the Process Go Together

*"Delivering consistent results the right way,
on time, first time, every time."*

What does Quality have to do with Project Management? The concept of quality is normally associated with "widgets" and their relationship to products, engineering, manufacturing and mass production. However, projects by definition are "unique endeavours" that don't fall into neatly defined environments associated with manufacturing activities. Even the conventional definitions of quality cannot be easily transferred to Project Management without a different approach and perspective.

The vast majority of accepted definitions for Quality include the following phrases:

- "Degree to which a set of inherent characteristic fulfills requirements"

- "Need or expectation that is stated, generally implied, or obligatory"

- "Conformance to specifications" and "implied fitness for use"

- "Drive towards customer satisfaction … "

The Project Manager's challenge is to understand the underlying principles and context for the definitions of Quality, and then to apply them in such a way that it will actually be helpful towards successful Project Management. Viewed from a Project Manager's perspective, Quality Management has the following four considerations:

1. Firstly, it deals with meeting specifications for the deliverables, end-products or services resulting from the project.

2. Secondly, the products and services must meet the test of suitability for their intended use.

3. Thirdly, Quality is a measure of the client's perception of value received from the project, and a measure of an overall experience of interaction and service during the project.

4. Finally, it also includes the quality of processes used to manage the project itself.

So, how does a Project Manager apply and practise Quality Management? One way is to think of it as having two dimensions; one related to the project and its products, and the other related to the processes for managing the product. As such, Quality Management addresses both the "What" and "How" of Project Management:

1. What is delivered: The quality of deliverables or end-product of the project

2. How it is managed: The Project Management process itself for managing the project

Quality for Project Deliverables

From a project perspective, the quality of deliverables starts with understanding the business need and drawing up a thorough requirements definition for the project. One cannot talk about quality if there is no common and clear agreement on requirements.

Quite often, it is not enough nor is it practical to have the client provide the requirements; what's required is for the Manager to understand the rationale for the requirements, and work with the client to formulate them.

Requirements may be implied, expressed, obvious, stated or, in some cases, "to be determined" depending on the type of the project. Good requirements are not about getting a signoff from the client; they are about mutual understanding, validation and confirmation of the expectations from the project.

The experienced Project Manager works with the client to drive the requirements in such a way that they are clear, unambiguous, testable, measurable and can be validated through the various phases of the project.

The implementation of Quality Management for a project generally consists of the following seven steps. The strategies and tools deployed for managing quality, as well as the level of expertise and specialization required for each step, will vary from industry to industry.

1. Define requirements

2. Prioritize and baseline the requirements

3. Establish measurement and validation criteria for each requirement

4. Develop a Quality Plan and integrate it into the Project Plan

5. Design the requirements into specifications and details for each deliverable

6. Develop test strategies, test plans, test tools, test data and test environment

7. Conduct tests and validate test results for agreed criteria during every phase of the project including design, protoypes, development, final assembly, operation etc.

Quality for Project Management Process

The process component of quality in Project Management defines the framework for managing quality for every project in the organization. As such, it does not address project-specific considerations, but it does lay down the ground rules to be consistently followed for managing projects.

- Use of a common framework and terminology of Project Quality Management

- Use of a Project Management Methodology (PMM) that sets the policies, processes, procedures and standards for managing projects

- Adoption of a recognized Quality System based on Total Quality Management (TQM), Six Sigma, Capability Maturity Model (CMM), Malcolm Baldrige Award Criteria or the ISO9001:2000 Quality Management Systems

Quality Management Systems

The choice of a Quality System is based on the type of industry, organizational goals, industry standards, and the portfolio of products and services. Any one of the Quality Systems will do the job, as it will benefit the organization by preventing errors, eliminating rework, improving delivery capability, optimizing processes and motivating team members.

It's not the quality system, but it's the discipline to follow the system that will determine the ultimate success of Quality Management. Figure 12 illustrates the principles associated with managing quality of project deliverables and project management processes, and their inter-dependence.

Quality Tools for Project Management

There are a large number of tools and techniques available for improving quality in Project Management. Although they are well known and commonly used in manufacturing, they can easily be adapted to the project environment. The tools can be used to capture data, document a process, monitor performance, analyze a situation, uncover a problem and find a resolution. They help us to take the guess work out of the picture, make visible the areas for potential improvement, and prompt us to take action.

Figure 12
Project & Process Quality View

```
                    Quality
                  Management
         ┌───────────┴───────────┐
    Project                  Project Mgt.
   Deliverables  ⟺           Processes
```

Unique for each Project
- Requirements Definition
- Requirements Baselining
- Measurement & Validation
- Project Quality Plan
- Test Strategy, Plan, Tools
- Test Data & Environment
- Verification of Test Results for Design, Prototype, Development, Final Assembly and Operation

Focus on Managing & Meeting the Client's expectations

Common to all Projects
- Methodology, Policies, Procedures, Standards & Tools
- Project Data Collection
- Measurement/ Analysis
  - Change Requests
  - Defect Detection
  - Defect Resolution
  - Estimating Accuracy
  - Client Satisfaction

Focus on Improving Processes & Continuous Improvement

The first step towards quality improvement is to collect relevant and meaningful data, and use simple charts and graphs to display and analyze it. Here's one way to group the tools:

- Data Collection tools – Check sheets, Concentration diagrams, Workflow diagrams

- Process Mapping tools - Process Maps, Value Stream mapping, Failure Modes and Effect Analysis (FMEA)

- Data Relationship tools - Pareto charts (known as the 80/20 rule), Run Charts (Time Plot), Control Charts (for process monitoring), Frequency Plots, Scatter plots

- Root Cause Analysis tools - Cause and Effect diagram, also known as Fishbone Diagram for problem solving, 5-Why Analysis

The big questions are "Why aren't the tools embraced by Project Managers?", and "How does one apply them to Project Management?" There are many excuses combined with the realities of Project Management: Lack of time and resources, pressure to deliver, management apathy, and above all, the reluctance to follow a disciplined process with standards for Project Management.

"I support standards, but my project is different", is a common saying often heard in many organizations and at different levels of management. Added to that is the lack of understanding regarding the relevance and use of tools for Project Management.

Measurement Analysis for Projects

Why not measure the key attributes for your projects with the Quality tools? After all, you can only improve what you can measure. Use a quality tool that helps you to do the job, and set up the foundation for continuous improvement with the measurement of the following:

Change Requests

Keep a log of Change Requests; Capture info on related stage, phase or step of the project; Analyze the type/ priority of request:

Critical (solution won't work otherwise), Mandatory (Required by Law), Medium (Required but can wait), Low (Would like to have

"Bells and Whistles"); Document days required to analyze, approve and implement.

How will you improve the processes for handling Change Requests?

Detection and Resolution of errors

Group errors into types or categories; Document type of error along with the phase/ process where it occurred; How and when it was detected; Time taken to analyze and rectify the error. Record cost of correcting the error.

How will you improve (a) the process for early detection of errors (b) response time for analyzing and resolving the errors (c) the overall cost of correcting the errors?

Specification Changes

Keep a log of changes to project requirements and specifications; Record by phase when the changes were identified; Investigate if there is a sudden surge; Analyze if change was caused due to incomplete or ambiguous requirements; Keep track of time spent in capturing requirements; Look for patterns.

How will you minimize the impact due to specification changes?

Estimating Accuracy

Capture schedule and cost estimates by work package, phase, milestone and the total project. Chart actual data and compare. Is the estimating accuracy improving or worsening? The pattern might indicate that the accuracy is very good for some team members and work packages, and not so good for others.

How will you improve the estimating process?

Client Signoffs and Satisfaction

The only tangibles that bind the Project Manager and the Client are the deliverables from the project. Keep track of the deliverables and signoffs. Chart the number of planned versus actual deliverables. Conduct a client satisfaction survey and analyze the results for improving client interaction. Document the number issues resolved with the client's participation. You may be required to improve your issue resolution process, but you cannot do it unless you have it in the first place.

What is an acceptable number of outstanding issues for the project? What will you do if the pattern shows an exceedingly high number of outstanding issues?

Quality Management is founded on the principle that all work consists of processes, and that they can be defined, measured and analyzed for improvement. Successful project organizations believe in this principle, and strive to internalize the use of Quality tools and techniques for improving their project management processes.

The Hierarchy of Success Criteria

How do you define success with respect to a project? Success is usually associated with project completion within time and budget to agreed scope. This definition is too constrained since it fails to take into account the objectives of the project and its impact on recipients, beneficiaries and end users of the project.

There is a need to look at project success in terms of its hierarchy as follows:

Level 1 – Completed within budget and time

Level 2 – Delivered to scope and agreed end products

Level 3 – Meets the client's overall quality expectations

Level 4 – Meets the business objectives and the primary purpose for which the project was intended

The levels indicate a hierarchy of criteria to assess the degree of success. The criteria for levels 1-3 are considered to be a pre-requisite for a successful project. But, what if the client and the end users are not satisfied with the outcome and the business objectives are not met? Conversely, what if the project exceeded the budget, or had a schedule slippage, or delivered less than the scope, but is perceived to be meeting the business need?

True project success is primarily associated with "business objectives" of the project. That is why it is imperative for the Project manager to focus on the business objectives. There is only one final test for evaluating the success of a project: Does it meet the business objectives? Does it fulfill the primary function for which it was intended? Is it being used by the end-user?

Project success, in the final analysis, is not merely driven by the considerations of scope, cost and time, but also by managing the client's expectations.

The Discipline of Debriefing

> *"Those who do not remember the past
> are condemned to repeat it."*
> *- George Santayana in The Life of Reason*

Debriefing is one of the most powerful tools to learn, modify and adapt Project Management processes based on the project team's experience. It is the only means to formally capture the lessons learnt with a focus on improving performance.

Debriefing is a process for reflection. It's not about assigning individual blame, but learning through an open dialogue. Debriefing sessions are ideally conducted at the end of each phase or on achievement of a significant milestone. They are facilitated workshops with participation from the team and stakeholders, and their only purpose is to understand what the team is good at and where it needs to improve.

Based on the results of debriefing, we continue to do more of what we are good at, and we aim to improve in those areas where we are lacking. A typical debriefing session includes the following:

1. What worked well and why?

2. What are the opportunities for improvement?

3. What could have been done differently?

4. What did the team learn?
   - Assessment re project deliverables
   - Assessment re Project Management process

5. Expected vs. Actual Business Benefits

6. Assessment of overall Project Benefits and Return on Investment (Recommended 3-4 months after implementation)

Project Managers who have no time for a debrief session forego a vital learning opportunity, and keep making the same mistakes over and over again from one project to another. Project Management is difficult, but it isn't going to be any easier if we don't learn from our experiences.

Chapter Summary

The principles and tools of Quality Management are an integral part of Project Management. Quality is viewed from two perspectives: Firstly, its application to managing the *"What"* of Quality Management for a specific project including its deliverables and end-products; and secondly, the *"How"* of Quality Management with its focus on the client, processes and customer satisfaction.

The "What" helps us to define, design, build and validate measurable quality attributes associated with project deliverables. The "How" helps us to continually improve the way we manage projects by focussing on learning, analyzing and improving the processes.

Although no two projects are the same, unlike in the manufacturing environment, there is still the commonality of processes and practices for managing them. Quality Management shows the way to profitable Project management by improving the common processes as well as meeting customer expectations.

Learning Lessons

Avoid the Rat Hole – Warning Signs

1. Requirements are ambiguous and cannot be measured or validated

2. There is no strategy to review or test requirements during each phase of the project

3. Requirements are continually evolving and there is too much rework

4. There is no awareness of quality management in the organization

5. Project pressures and priorities justify bypassing the process

Catch the Rainbow – Best Practices

1. Adopt a "process" view of Project Management; Define the processes

2. Educate management, client and the project team on the Quality initiative

3. Adopt the seven quality tools for monitoring project variables

4. Monitor cost of quality – Conformance and non-conformances

5. Continually validate Project objectives and Team Confidence

6. Maintain project records for continual improvement

7. Strive for "Every deliverable on time, first time every time"

8. Develop a balanced score card for the project; keep it simple

9. Hold Post implementation audits, lessons learned sessions

10. Institute customer satisfaction measures and conduct post-implementation surveys

11. Maintain history of project data for reference and use it

12. Diligently follow the process for managing projects – You cannot improve a process by avoiding it!

13 people make projects happen

Don't Let Your Team Run Out of Steam

*"Men work together", I told him from the heart,
Whether they work together or apart."*
- Robert Frost

Project Management is defined as the art and science of getting work done with the active cooperation of other people including Senior Management, Project Sponsors(s), Customers, End-users, Stakeholders, Team Members, Sub-contractors, Vendors and Consultants.

Professional Project Management is subject to increased industry pressures from accelerated implementations, restructuring and downsizing, mergers and acquisitions, faster technology obsolescence, and the use of new and unproven technologies. Furthermore, the project environment itself is rapidly changing with the use of distributed and virtual teams, as organizations implement new "Projectized" cultures.

The challenge for the Project Manager consists of attracting the right resources, forming a cohesive team, keeping the team motivated, meeting individual aspirations and getting the work done – all within scope, cost, time, and customer satisfaction! How should we meet the challenge?

Creating successful teams requires a conscious and deliberate investment of time. Teams are built around four basic principles that recognize the importance of Team Structure, Team Process,

Team Culture and Team Politics. They need to embrace a common purpose, develop and follow a set of processes, believe in and build a common set of values and culture, and learn the art of influencing others to achieve the project outcome.

We can begin by looking at successful teams and evaluate what made them highly effective and successful. There are five key ingredients:

Characteristics of Effective Project Teams

1. Everyone knows who is in charge

2. There is a clear understanding of the project objectives

3. There are clear expectations of each person's role & responsibilities

4. Team members believe in a common purpose and have a results-oriented outlook

5. There is a high degree of cooperation and collaboration among the team members

Central to the formation of teams is the concept of a well defined team structure, team process, team culture and team politics. The vast majority of project failures can be attributed to people issues: Lack of understanding, lack of motivation, lack of commitment and lack of purpose.

The presence of an enthusiastic, motivated team that passionately believes in a common purpose is invaluable for achieving project success. Team spirit is formed at a personal level by the sharing of culture, values and beliefs set by an organization.

Figure 13-A illustrates the principles for building an effective team and how the Project Manager can meet the challenge with the following Golden Rules:

Managing Successful Teams – Ten Golden Rules

1. Develop a Project Organization

A project exists to satisfy a business need and it must have a customer. Use the Project Organization to clearly define the sponsor, customer, project manager, stakeholders and team members. Develop roles and responsibilities and identify names for each. Absence of a specific name or individual for each role should raise a red flag. Use the project organization chart to define what's expected of them. Teams need an organization structure to operate smoothly, and the existence of a well-defined structure reduces stress.

Figure 13-A

Project Team View

Project Management is ...
the art and science of "Getting Work Done"
with the active cooperation of your project team

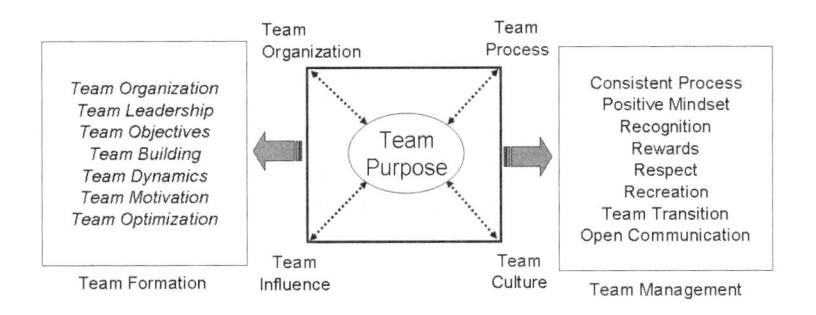

Team Organization
Team Leadership
Team Objectives
Team Building
Team Dynamics
Team Motivation
Team Optimization

Team Organization
Team Process
Team Purpose
Team Influence
Team Culture

Consistent Process
Positive Mindset
Recognition
Rewards
Respect
Recreation
Team Transition
Open Communication

Team Formation
Team Management

Invest in building and nurturing your Project Team

2. Formulate a Team Purpose

Teams need a common vision, purpose and goal for their success. Guide your team through the "Form, Storm, Norm and Perform" steps. Encourage the team to develop its own rules, norms and processes for effective functioning. Reinforce the team purpose throughout the project. It serves no purpose to have a team if the team members don't know, or passionately believe in the purpose.

3. Hold a formal kick-off meeting

Share and establish a common understanding of the project goals during the project kickoff. Present a high level overview and major milestones with dependencies and the critical path. Invite a senior executive to demonstrate management support for the project. Introduce your team members and let the show begin!

4. Insulate Team from Organizational Politics

The Project Manager's job is to remove the obstacles that prevent team members from doing their jobs. Establish a process for escalating and resolving issues. Protect and support your team. As previously stated, a Project Manager can only delegate responsibility, but cannot abdicate it. Organizational politics is a fact of life. Manage internal team politics as well as external project politics. Play politics with the objective of leveraging it to influence the desired project outcome.

5. Optimize Team Effort

Successful teams operate at two levels - Individuals Maximize and Teams Optimize. At the individual level, "What's in it for me?" (WIIFM) is the first question. Work to change that into "How can we achieve it together?" and gain commitment. Establish a facilitation process and encourage team decisions through consensus. Commitment begins with active participation and involvement in the decision making process.

6. Encourage and Facilitate Open Communication

Open communication means a culture based on the exchange and sharing of information in a non-threatening environment. That's the way to build trust. Many organizations practice a culture of fear or intimidation, and that will certainly drive the project into a rat hole. As a project Manager, you need to get all the relevant news – the only bad news is the one that comes as a surprise or doesn't come at all. No news is bad news! Have a formal and structured communication process that includes weekly status reports and "one on one" reviews. Ascertain and reinforce a team member's confidence during the reviews.

7. Institutionalize Positive Mindset – Team Culture

A positive mindset results from a sense of ownership and the satisfaction of making a worthwhile contribution. Focus on what's expected of your team members, and encourage them to define how best to do it. Guide the team, but don't micro-manage. Make meetings productive. Focus on problem resolution, not on assigning blame. Conduct professional meetings, get feedback on the meeting content and process, and continually improve the meeting process.

8. Practice the 5 R's

Respect, Recognition, Rewards, Rest and Recreation – these are the five characteristics of successful teams. When everyone practises them, you know you have a cohesive, motivated and high performance team. Respect acknowledges the need for, and acceptance of the team member. Motivation feeds on recognition. Plan and budget for the five Rs. Establish frequent milestones with challenging but realistic and achievable goals. Celebrate significant achievements. Always thank, congratulate and recognize team members for their specific contribution to the project. When the dust settles, this is what they will remember and cherish.

9. Implement Consistent & Predictable Processes

Process ensures predictability in the way the team interacts. You have a limited set of tools to get the project done. The tools of your trade are agendas, minutes, status reports, signoffs, review meetings, project plans, charts and documentation. Methodologies and processes provide discipline, consistency and predictability in your projects. Leverage the tools to move the project forward, and train the team to use them effectively.

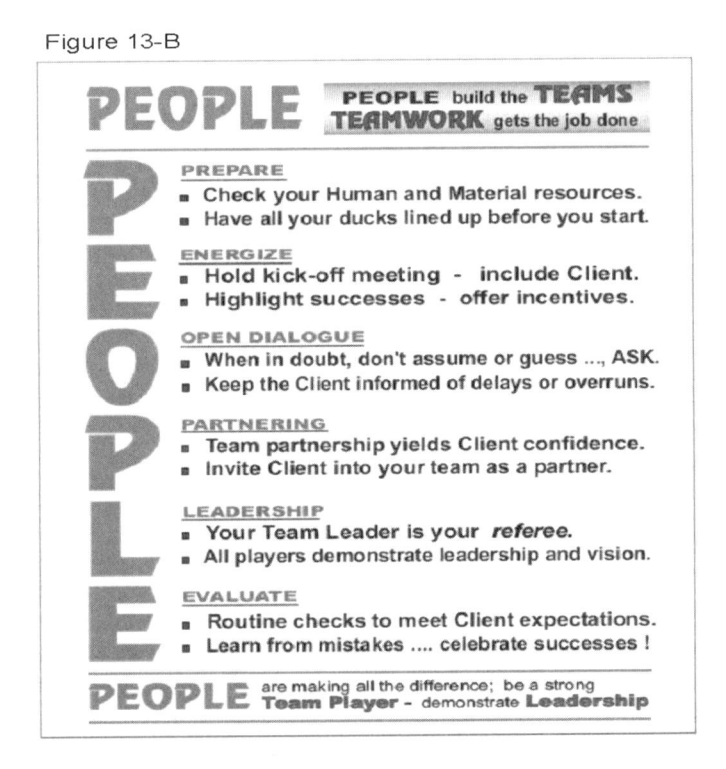

Figure 13-B

PEOPLE PEOPLE build the TEAMS
TEAMWORK gets the job done

P — PREPARE
- Check your Human and Material resources.
- Have all your ducks lined up before you start.

E — ENERGIZE
- Hold kick-off meeting - include Client.
- Highlight successes - offer incentives.

O — OPEN DIALOGUE
- When in doubt, don't assume or guess ..., ASK.
- Keep the Client informed of delays or overruns.

P — PARTNERING
- Team partnership yields Client confidence.
- Invite Client into your team as a partner.

L — LEADERSHIP
- Your Team Leader is your *referee*.
- All players demonstrate leadership and vision.

E — EVALUATE
- Routine checks to meet Client expectations.
- Learn from mistakes .... celebrate successes !

PEOPLE are making all the difference; be a strong **Team Player** - demonstrate **Leadership**

10. Transition the Team graciously

You have invested effort and time to build the team. Don't let it vanish abruptly at the end of the project. Identify responsibilities for support and warranties. Provide feedback to team members on their project performance. Hold a "Lessons Learnt" or post-implementation review. Finally, organize a small celebration with key stakeholders for a formal project closure. That's one way to avoid being stuck with an "ongoing" project!

Figure 13-B illustrates the role of Project Mangers in building effective teams, and lists guidelines for creating and sustaining teams where "People Make Projects Happen".

Chapter Summary

Effective teams are crucial to the success of a project. Team building starts with the Project Manager who provides leadership, practices soft skills, demonstrates commitment, encourages self-empowerment, and above all, nurtures teamwork and client relationships. These skills enable to Project Manager to:

1. Develop and manage workable processes based on available resources

2. Delegate, motivate and manage people to the peak of their abilities

3. Perform under pressure to meet critical timings without sacrificing quality

4. Manage unexpected changes as they happen and welcome them as 'opportunities'

5. Communicate and work as a team to satisfy the customer's expectations

People make projects happen! Build your team with the Ten Golden Rules.

Learning Lessons

Avoid the Rat Hole – Warning Signs

1. Project goals are not clearly understood or accepted
2. Roles and Responsibilities of team members are not defined
3. There is no formal Team Structure
4. Team members lack enthusiasm and commitment
5. Poor leadership and poor communication
6. High Turnover of Project Team Members
7. Dysfunctional Behaviour among team members

Catch the "Pot of Gold" - Best Practices

1. Practice the 5Rs

    - Respect, Recognition, Rewards, Rest and Recreation

2. Energize your team and the client
3. Hold open dialogue with team members and the client
4. Follow problem-solving and decision making processes
5. Focus on the final objective with leadership and vision

14 it won't happen if you can't communicate

Communication Skills and Tools for Survival

"No News is Bad News"

How do you actually get your work done when working with a team of people? Not by swinging a baseball bat at the team or trying to settle issues in the parking lot! The only thing you have at your disposal is your superior skill to communicate effectively. And, strangely enough, this is one skill, the ability to influence and communicate, that most Project Managers lack!

Project Management is one hundred percent about communication. The outstanding Project Manager spends 70%-80% of his time and effort towards managing project communication – upwards with senior management, sideways with the client and stakeholders, and downwards with the project team. This is the most important skill for a Project Manager. Communication is the least understood and appreciated aspect of Project Management. And yet, it is the only vehicle at the PM's disposal to drive the project.

Project Managers are required to deal with new organization structures that are getting flatter by the day. They introduce new models of matrix management that do not strictly conform to the traditional concepts of command, obedience, control, hierarchy, loyalty and rules. They require that Project Managers get things done through people over whom they have no direct authority or control. With Project Management, the name of the game and the ground rules for managing people change.

This is how I used to feel when I started my PM career: Why bother with agendas, meetings, minutes, status reports, presentations, brain-storming and problem-solving? What a monumental waste of time! All so unnecessary, making us fall further behind schedule. Just leave my team and me alone so that we can get the job done. That is a typical engineering or technology view of Project Management.

The Goal of Project Communication

The goal of every project communication interaction should be to advance and drive the project towards achieving the intended outcome. Easier said than done! There are diversions. Organizations change, technology evolves, the market fluctuates, and the client's understanding of the project undergoes modifications. If none of these things changed, if everything remained static, if every single activity happened as originally planned, if, if, if . . . then, we might as well forget about Project Management and look for another profession.

But change is constant. Projects are affected by changes to the internal and external environment, and they also introduce major changes in the organization. Projects impact the way work is done – people, process and technology. Project Management is about managing change in organizations and the tool for managing change is communication.

Communication is the lifeline of the project. It can make or break the project. It helps the Project Manager to sell, probe, settle, advance, and negotiate the various ideas and issues in a changing environment. It helps to set the client's expectations and deliver successful projects. No news is bad news when it comes to Project Management.

Modes of Communication

Communication occurs in many ways: Written, verbal, non-verbal, conference calls and quite often through electronic devices. Successful Project Managers know how to leverage the various modes of communication to manage the project. They practice their communication skills and they leverage communication tools. Figure 14 lists a summary of the modes of communication that are commonly practised by Project Managers.

Communication is not complete or successful if it hasn't achieved the desired result or the expected outcome. It goes through all of the five stages – it must be sent, received, acknowledged, understood and acted upon to be considered as successful. Merely sending the communication is no guarantee that it will achieve the desired outcome.

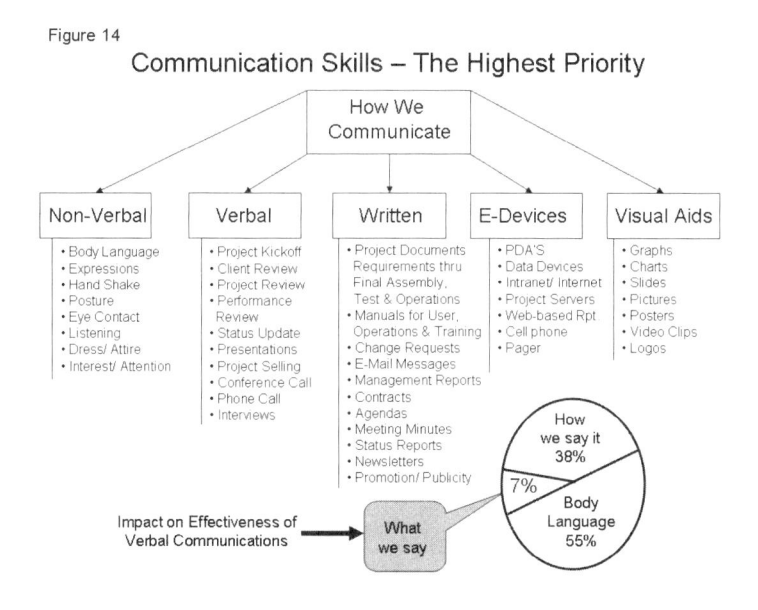

Figure 14

Communication Skills – The Highest Priority

```
                        How We
                      Communicate
```

Non-Verbal	Verbal	Written	E-Devices	Visual Aids
• Body Language	• Project Kickoff	• Project Documents	• PDA'S	• Graphs
• Expressions	• Client Review	Requirements thru	• Data Devices	• Charts
• Hand Shake	• Project Review	Final Assembly,	• Intranet/ Internet	• Slides
• Posture	• Performance	Test & Operations	• Project Servers	• Pictures
• Eye Contact	Review	• Manuals for User,	• Web-based Rpt.	• Posters
• Listening	• Status Update	Operations & Training	• Cell phone	• Video Clips
• Dress/ Attire	• Presentations	• Change Requests	• Pager	• Logos
• Interest/ Attention	• Project Selling	• E-Mail Messages		
	• Conference Call	• Management Reports		
	• Phone Call	• Contracts		
	• Interviews	• Agendas		
		• Meeting Minutes		
		• Status Reports		
		• Newsletters		
		• Promotion/ Publicity		

Impact on Effectiveness of Verbal Communications → What we say

How we say it 38%
7%
Body Language 55%

Written Communications

Written communications are the backbone of project management. "What's not documented doesn't exist" is a common saying among Project Managers. It can be broadly grouped into two categories:

Project Documents

Business Requirements, Statement of Work, User Specifications, Design documents, Operations Manual, Training Guide, User Manual, policies, procedures, project standards, Contracts and Warranty & Support. These documents need to be written in simple, clear and unambiguous language. Once developed, these rarely change. If a change occurs, it would usually result in a Change Request.

Working Documents

They facilitate day to day communication. These include memos, announcements, emails, procedures, meeting agenda, minutes of meetings, status reports, signoffs, newsletters and faxes etc. Good business writing skills, timeliness and clarity of the text/message are critical.

Verbal Communication

Proficiency in verbal communication is critical for meetings, interviews, project reviews, status update, client and management presentations, stakeholder meetings, project selling, phone calls, voice mail and conference calls. What you say is as important as how you say it. The content and the medium go together.

Non-verbal Communication

We also rely extensively on our non-verbal communication, often known as body language. This includes facial expressions, mannerisms, posture, eye contact, gestures and appearance. Body language comprises everything except the spoken word, and it reflects the subtle messages conveyed without words.

According to communication experts, the impact we make on others is a function of what we say, how we say it and the body language we use during communication.

- What we say – the words themselves – has 7% impact on communication

- How we say it – voice, tone, speed, pauses etc. – has 38% impact

- The Body language we use – everything except the words – has 55% impact

In other words, close to 93% of our communication can practically happen without using actual words. From a Project Management perspective, it is safe to say that 60-80% of our message is communicated through our body language. Body language counts!

E-Devices for Communication

A significant portion of our communication includes the use of new technologies and tools such as Personal Digital Assistants (PDAs), data devices, cell phones, pagers, webinars, and the use of web-enabled project management tools for documentation and reporting.

Due to the ease and speed of communication offered by these tools, their use has spread like wild fire in most organizations. It is up to the Project Manager to learn to use them selectively and effectively. Keep in mind, though, the tools cannot be a substitute for formal interaction and communication on the project.

Communication Challenges

The realities in organizations and project communication are:

1. *Messages get interpreted, re-interpreted or simply lost in translation.*

    This can happen due to the sheer number of players and multiple communication channels. Add to that the complexity arising from individual personality, attitude, agenda, game plan perceptions and motivation with respect to the project. Language, however clearly spoken or written, is still an imperfect medium for achieving 100% success in communication.

2. *Organization culture forces people to be optimistic.*

    Many organizations have an "institutionalized" project culture that demands only positive and optimistic feedback on their projects. Such a culture refuses to acknowledge the existence of risks and potential problems, and demands that the Project Manager put a positive twist on them, regardless of the consequences.

3. *No one likes to be the bearer of bad news.*

    Some organizations have a culture of fear or intimidation that has filtered all the way down from the top. Such a culture thrives on, and expects a "yes" mentality from its team members, and contributes to a threatening environment. Team members in this culture keep their heads down rather than voice the issues. No one wants to know the facts and real issues until, of course, the project turns into a disaster.

4. *Communication Overload leads to Chaos, Confusion and Consternation*

    The ease of communicating with various tools can result in over communication. As team size increases, so do the potential channels of communication. In many projects, there is often a lack of protocol for communication. The end result is wasted time, duplication of effort, and detracting people from doing what they are supposed to do. For communication to be effective, it must be clear, concise and complete, and it must be specific and meaningful to the recipients.

5. *Politics, Politics, Politics ..... a fact of life.*

   Project Communication is subject to, and suffers from the state of organizational politics, especially when it is the only game in town. In such organizations, teamwork and trust are on the back-burner until departmental or individual rivalries are settled. Politics, when practiced in the negative sense, leads to dysfunctional organizations.

   Outstanding Project Managers think of politics in a positive sense, and practice it as an art for influencing people to achieve the project goals. True politics is, *"Having the organizational savvy to get your ideas and recommendations accepted".*

What should the Project Manager do?

1. Understand the role of the Project Manager. It is to help team members do their job by providing direction and coaching as required.

2. Create an environment where team members can identify and escalate potential problems and their concerns without fear or reprisals

3. Support the team and demonstrate confidence in the team. "Generals that support their people generally win wars, and they win the loyalty of their troupes."

4. Stop, look, listen and think – Ask questions, get feedback, solicit ideas, monitor morale, validate commitments, involve the team, coach individual members, insulate the team from organizational politics, say "Thank You".

Chapter Summary

The only way things get done on a project is through effective, timely and successful communication. This is where the rubber hits the road! There is no other option. Successful Project Managers work hard at developing their communication skills and learning how to use the various communication tools to manage the project.

They know how to leverage the multitude of reports, charts, minutes, signoffs, meetings, conference calls etc. to advance the project towards its goal. They know how to intervene at the appropriate time to prevent the ship from sinking. They also understand that what we wish to communicate is as important as how we communicate it.

The content and the process of communication go hand in hand.

Learning Lessons

Avoid the Rat Hole – Warning Signs

1. Communication is not in the client's or user's language

2. Too much communication but no focus, follow up and action

3. Too much dependence on tools results in confusion rather than create understanding

4. Team members engage themselves in communication with the sole objective of protecting their careers or assigning blame on someone else, commonly known as the CYA attitude

5. No one knows the completion criteria – when is the project DONE?

6. Putting a positive spin regardless of the facts is part of the culture or it is expected

Catch the "Pot of Gold" - Best Practices

1. Issue weekly Project Status reports & Monthly newsletter

2. Have a checklist of deliverables and obtain incremental signoffs

3. Validate that the communication is complete

4. Keep the "macro" view and the big picture visible

5. Provide visuals re project organization, dependency chart, milestone completion etc. and post them in the project war room

6. Maintain perspective - Don't lose sight of the forest for the trees

15 manage your soft skills

The "How" Goes with the "What"

"The most important thing in communication is hearing what isn't said."
- Peter F. Drucker

Project Management is about getting things done. In this role, the Project Manager is expected to be proficient in applying all the skills that one can muster to keep the project moving in the right direction. What used to be known as the "Kick Butt" style of Project Management has now evolved into a far more complex role. In this new role, the Project Manager is not merely a leader and an implementer, but a facilitator, negotiator, problem-solver and change agent all at the same time!

The skill sets required to effectively perform this new role are considered to be "Soft Skills" and can be grouped as follows from a Project Manager's perspective:

1. *Communication Skills* for Email Management, Conference Calling and Voice Mail

2. *Interpersonal Skills* for Conflict Resolution, Negotiations and Networking Relationships

3. *Development Skills* for Effective Listening , Coaching and Mentoring

4. *Public Speaking Skills* for Meeting Management and Presentations

5. *Creativity Skills* for Facilitation, Problem Solving and Decision Making

In spite of the abundance of training, the development of soft skills continues to be a major area of concern for Project Managers. Most Project Managers are aware of these skills, but many fail to apply and practice them as an integral part of their management discipline and style. As illustrated in Figure 15, here are some key areas for developing soft skills and the reasons why you need to develop them.

Writing Skills

Project Management consists of creating, distributing, processing and updating hundreds of documents from requirements definition to project completion. The paperwork keeps the project moving, be it a Statement of Work, Design Specification, Test Strategy, Status Report or Minutes of Meeting.

The effectiveness of project communication depends on the clarity and simplicity of documentation, and writing is the universal basic and formal means of exchanging project information. In many cases, the cause for project failures can be directly attributed to a lack of writing skills that result in project teams working with vague and ambiguous requirements

The Email culture continues to have a powerful influence on writing skills. In many organizations, Email is the primary and dominant means of communication today. According to industry experts, 70% of executives use email as their primary method of communication followed by meetings and phone calls. Effective writing skills are essential regardless of the means used for communication. Yet, few Project Managers know how to write effectively or deal with email overload!

Meeting Management Skills

A Project Manager typically attends 2-3 meetings every day. That adds up to 40-60 meetings every month! Productive meetings require ground rules, clear objectives, meeting agenda, team participation and formal adjournment. Meetings should conclude with feedback from participants on content and process of the meeting.

Experienced Project Managers make effective use of meetings, issue action-oriented minutes within one day of the meeting, and follow up on a regular basis. A favourite expression among Project managers is, *"the one who controls the minutes, controls the project."*

With an increased trend towards tele-commuting, job-sharing, virtual teams, outsourcing and off-shoring, many organizations conduct their meetings with conference calls. The challenges associated with a conference call are quite unique as they need strong facilitation, directed participation and strict adherence to ground rules for conducting the meeting. Experienced Project Managers know how to conduct a successful conference call.

Presentation Skills

An essential ingredient of project leadership is the ability to make effective presentations. There are many occasions and reasons that call for project presentations. They include launching a project, holding a kickoff, updating a client, persuading a stakeholder, requesting an approval, asking for funds, selling an idea, motivating a team or just sharing information.

Every presentation puts the Project Manager on display to be evaluated by an audience. The successful Project Manager treats presentations as the means to sell, convince or motivate by demonstrating control, confidence, leadership and commitment to the project.

Facilitation skills

Projects exist in an environment that consists of organizational conflicts, competing interests, varying priorities and individual differences. These factors often introduce many twists and turns in the path of a project and impact its progress.

An experienced Project Manager brings all parties together, and provides a framework for discussion with the objective of achieving understanding and consensus. The Project Manager needs to possess strong facilitation skills to resolve internal differences, build effective teams and get everyone on board throughout the life cycle of the project.

Figure 15

Soft Skills and Project Management
Communication ..... the only vehicle available to drive the project !

Develop your soft skills

- Status Reports
- Agenda
- Minutes
- Action Items
- Escalations
- Newsletters

Written Skills	Verbal & Non-verbal
Presentation	Meeting Management
Facilitation	Negotiations
Interpersonal	Team Building
Coaching & Mentoring	Networking
Effective Listening	Conflict Management
Decision-making	Problem-solving

- Project "Selling"
- Kick-off Meetings
- Status Meetings
- Project Reviews
- Design Reviews
- Client Updates

- Dependency Charts
- Change Orders
- Specifications
- Project Docs
- Completion Report
- Sign-offs

- Email
- Voice Mail
- Intranet
- Conference Calls
- Net Meetings
- One-on-one

"80% of Project Management is Communication"
Develop the Skills and use the tools for effective communication

Problem Solving Skills

A project can be viewed as a collection of ongoing problems that need to be resolved. Everyone has a different perception or version of the problem and an opinion regarding how to resolve it, and who should be blamed for it. There is pressure to address the symptoms of a problem and implement a "quick-fix" even though there is no agreement on the problem to be solved.

The Project Manager is responsible for ensuring that problems are identified, defined, analyzed and resolved. The Project Manager's role is to apply effective problem-solving skills, help the team to understand the problem and identify root causes for further resolution. Chapter 12 "Quality is What the Client Experiences" lists a variety of problem solving tools.

Decision Making Skills

The Project Manager is constantly faced with making decisions related to changes, escalations, priorities, resources, risks and technologies. How does one arrive at a decision that is practical, sound and viable? The Project Manager achieves this by following a team process for analysis and synthesis of available data, and getting the team to participate in discussing alternatives and their impact.

A good decision making process is ideally based on arriving at a consensus. Decision taking, however, is an act by an individual based on facts and intuition, and accepting responsibility for the consequences. The Project Manager follows a decision making process, and takes responsibility for whatever decision is taken.

Conflict Resolution skills

Conflict originates due to a real or perceived gap in expectations between two parties. It may arise due to various factors related to people, personalities, attitudes, project constraints, ambiguous roles, stressful environment and the inherent bureaucracy and complexity of modern organizations. The existence of a conflict doesn't mean that there is something inherently wrong with the situation.

In most cases, it is the result of something that has gone wrong with respect to assumptions, interpretations, expectations, and understandings among the involved parties. The Project Manager recognizes the conflict, deals with it and uses the opportunity to strengthen teamwork in the process. A conflict ignored or wished away is an invitation for an unpleasant surprise on the project.

Negotiation skills

A Project Manager is constantly engaged in negotiations regarding the many factors that affect the scope, schedule or cost of a project. They include negotiations with management, customer, stakeholders and team members. A routine process for getting a change request approved by the client, with its resultant impact on schedule and cost, often results in a complex negotiation process.

Acquiring the right resources and holding on to them turns out to be an intense negotiation particularly when the resources belong to another department or organization. Every step - starting from finalizing requirements to obtaining a final sign-off - involves negotiations. The vast majority of job descriptions today require that the Project Manager must be an able negotiator.

Networking Skills

Networking is the art of building relationships with people. At the heart of networking is the individual's attitude based on helping others when possible, and seeking help when necessary. This ability to persuade and influence people is an essential skill for Project Managers. It requires an understanding of how an organization really works, and how people interact, influence and make decisions.

Networking pierces through the formal structure and enables one to build relationships based on empathy, friendships, mutual understanding, support and trust. It facilitates access to right individuals when support is needed for the project. Successful

Project Managers develop a relationship with each person on the project team and maintain it throughout the duration of the project and beyond.

Success in Project Management is a function of Knowledge and the network of Relationships: *Success = Knowledge x Relationships.*

Effective Listening skills

Good listening skills are at the core of successful and effective communications. Why is listening difficult? There is a physiological reason: it has to do with the way the human brain works. Our normal speech consists of 150-200 words per minute, while the brain has the capacity to process speech at the rate of 500-750 words per minute. It is this excess capacity that hijacks our concentration, and makes listening difficult.

Listening is an acquired skill that is diligently learnt and nurtured by giving undivided attention to the other person, asking open ended questions ("Help me understand"; "How would you deal with ... "; "Give me an example ... ") and showing genuine interest in the subject being discussed.

Coaching and Mentoring Skills

The ability to develop people is a key expectation of the Project Manager. The project environment presents an ideal opportunity for team members to develop their skills and competencies both in the technical and soft skills areas. Project Managers who take a genuine interest in the development of people in their teams will gain their respect and confidence.

It is the experience of learning something new, with the challenge of accomplishing something great that motivates team members. Project Managers facilitate the process by coaching, mentoring and recognizing the strengths of each team member and harnessing those strengths throughout the project.

Chapter Summary

The Project Manager's success is closely tied with the maturity of soft skills that include Communication, Interpersonal, Developmental, Speaking and Creativity skills. In the absence of these skills, the project deteriorates into a dysfunctional team. Project Management is essentially the coordination of human interaction and activities, and it happens only with the conscious learning and application of people skills.

In most cases, the root causes of project failures have to do with human failures – failure of communication, failure of leadership, failure of understanding and the failure of imagination. The effective use of soft skills can help the Project Manager to overcome the human aspect of project failures.

Learning Lessons

Avoid the Rat Hole – Warning Signs

1. The Project Manager views Soft Skills as irrelevant and "touchy-feely" stuff

2. The Project Managers style is based on "I talk, you listen" or "I tell, you do" approach

3. The project is perceived to be solely a technology challenge

4. Everyone believes that meetings are a waste of time

5. Team members don't know how decisions are made

6. There is a lack of clear, concise and comprehensive documentation

Catch the Pot of Gold – Best Practices

1. Develop an awareness of the benefit of soft skills among team members

2. Adopt a team process that will encourage the use of soft skills

3. Develop and practice the soft skills until they are internalized and become second nature

4. Coach team members to develop and apply soft skills

5. Engage actively in making presentations to client, management and project team

16 doing the right thing for your project

Professionalism and Project Management

"Your reputation is only as good as your last project."

A Project Manager has obligations and loyalties towards many constituencies that are associated with the project. The Project Manager will find it impossible to function effectively without making a conscious effort to meet the obligations and balance the loyalties with respect to the project, the profession, the product, the client, the employer, the team and the stakeholders.

To meet this challenge, the Project Manager follows a set of guidelines to ensure professionalism and exercises the skills as outlined in the previous chapter. Professionalism is built around personal integrity, and the Project Manager uses the skills to advance professionalism as illustrated in Figure 16-A.

The Seven Loyalties of the Project Manager

1. **Loyalty to the Client**

    - Keeps the client engaged and informed throughout the project

    - Understands the client's business needs

    - Communicates in the language of the client's business

    - Ensures that the business needs are met

- Advises the client about management of change
- Manages the client's expectations – no surprises!

2. **Loyalty to the Profession**

    - Follows guidelines for professional ethics by organizations such as the PMI
    - Accepts responsibility for the project and its results
    - Reports project status objectively, based on facts
    - Avoids situations that may result in compromising one's integrity
    - Does the right thing that is consistent with the legal and financial reporting requirements for the project

Figure 16-A
The Professional Project Manager Loyalties and Obligations

- **Customer** – Focus on Client Relationship
- **Professionalism** – Driven by Ethics & Integrity
- **Project** – Committed to Project Objectives
- **Deliverables** – Achieving Product & Process Quality
- **Employer** – Building Trust & Confidence
- **Project Team** – Coaching & Building Teamwork
- **Stakeholders** – Dealing with Interests & Concerns
- **Self-Development** – Improving Skills & Competencies

3. **Loyalty to the Project**

    - Believes in the project and demonstrates passion for the project
    - Performs due diligence throughout the project life cycle
    - Follows a consistent and predictable process for managing the project
    - Promises only what can be delivered within the constraints of scope, time & cost
    - Knows when to ask for help

4. **Loyalty to the Product and Deliverables**

    - Follows industry standards and guidelines
    - Builds quality into project deliverables from requirements through final test
    - Conducts thorough testing at each phase or stage of the project
    - Ensures that the product meets the client's stated and implied needs
    - Provides complete documentation re technical, operations, training and support aspects of the product

5. **Loyalty to the Employer**

    - Protects employer's interests
    - Keeps management informed of risks and alternatives
    - Escalates issues for resolution

- Manages project cost and profitability
- Understands the employer's organization and its business
- Develops an effective network across the organization

6. **Loyalty to the Project Team**

    - Demonstrates confidence in team members
    - Provides coaching and mentoring for team members
    - Insulates team members from external politics
    - Takes responsibility for the team's performance
    - Promotes open communication, teamwork and harmony

7. **Loyalty to the Stakeholders**

    - Maintains awareness of project's impact on stakeholders
    - Addresses stakeholders' interests and concerns
    - Keeps stakeholders informed of project direction
    - Develops trusting relationships based on open dialogue
    - Practices an "inclusive" style of management

Project Management and SOX

The passing of the Serbanes-Oxley Act (SOX) in the United States underlines how the Project Management landscape has become very regulatory & competitive with its focus on transparency. The Act was instituted to prevent the repetition of major corporate and financial scandals associated with companies such as Enron,

Worldcom and many others. It applies to all corporate enterprises in the United Sates and their international subsidiaries and operations around the world.

What is the impact of SOX on Project Management and how can it be applied?

Figure 16-B
Project Management, SOX and ISO 9001

	Serbanes-Oxley Act (SOX)	ISO 9001-2000
Scope	US Corporations and their subsidiaries world-wide	Any organization around the world
Type	Regulatory Act by US Congress with focus on Audit Power, Audit Requirements, Strict Penalties & Personal/Mgt. Responsibility	Developed by International Standards Organization (ISO); Administered by registered ISO auditors.
Purpose	Minimize fraud by conformance to Financial Reporting rules	Promote "Quality-Driven" organizations
Impact	Violation may result in a fine or jail sentence	Voluntarily adopted to improve Quality
Project Mgt Relevance	Ensure compliance re the Seven Pillars of Transparency	Quality as it relates to Project Deliverables and Project Mgt. Processes
Focus	Focus on preventing fraud particularly with respect to Financial Reporting	Focus on continuous improvement ..."Doing it right the first time, every time, all the time"
Outcome	Impacts content and quality of reporting. Also applies to external auditors who are responsible for the audit.	Impacts organization's culture including mgt & employee commitment, policies, procedures, operations and client service
Output	Extensive documentation to primarily satisfy regulations. May not necessarily enhance Quality	Process-oriented documents that define, measure and improve the overall conduct of a business

The SOX Act has four key elements that cover new Audit Requirements, Personal Power, Audit Power and Stricter Penalties. The Act affects all "C" level executives such as the Chief Executive Office (CEO), Chief Financial Officer (CFO), Chief Information Office (CIO), Chief Accounting Officer (CAO) and other executives with similar roles and responsibilities in the organization. It also applies to External Auditors who are responsible for auditing the company's accounting standards and practices.

The SOX Act, according to Section 404 of the Act, stipulates that the management executive is responsible for the validity of data, statistics and numbers reported about the project, as well as the process by which the numbers were obtained.

The SOX Act is significant to a Project Manager's responsibilities because it expects and ensures the existence of, and adherence to the following *seven pillars of transparency* with respect to Project Management.

Ensuring Transparency for Project Management

The *Seven Pillars of Transparency* as they apply to Project Management can be interpreted as follows:

1. **Terms & Terminology** as it refers to Project Management Methodology

2. **Project Management Process** includes the existence of standard policies, procedures, checkpoint reviews, phase approvals

3. **Audit Trail Capability** consists of verifiable audit trails of budget and actuals for schedule and costs, and any changes to the project scope, cost and schedule

4. **Compliance** to industry, regulatory and accounting standards in relation to the project's technical, financial and cost management aspects

5. **Enforcement** with the evidence to prove that project management governance, methodology and process is enforced by management and adhered to, by the project team

6. **Measurement** includes consistent and reliable methods for measuring, reporting and communicating information about the project to all stakeholders

7. **Accountability** requires a single point of accountability and responsibility for the project

Impact of SOX on Project Managers

For each one of the seven items listed above, it is expected that the organization has clear documentation with respect to Who, What, Where, Why, When, and How. The impact of SOX on Project Management is that Project Managers will need to:

1. Plan the required work for project management and oversight

2. Negotiate with management for additional funding

3. Create awareness of SOX among project team members

4. Develop intelligent data regarding Analytics and Measurement

5. Maintain focus on project objectives and Return on Investment

6. Establish performance standards and validation procedures

7. Institute Program Management for multi-project environments for governance, processes and integration with other business functions and systems

8. Implement a strong measurable process for project budgeting, allocation, planning, commitment and fund balances regarding Total, Planned, Committed, Earned and Paid categories of funds

9. Sub-certify every step taken and document every deviation

10. Be vigilant! Start by having a process NOW!

ISO 9001 and SOX

While the ISO 9001 standards are adopted voluntarily by organizations, the SOX Act is enforced as a regulation. The former emphasizes customer focus with a commitment to continuous improvement and delivering the right product or service "first time, every time and on time", while the latter is aimed at preventing fraud by instituting the rules for reporting and ensuring transparency in organizations. Figure 16-B summarizes the common factors and key differences between ISO 9001 and SOX with respect to Project Management.

ISO 9001 emphasizes the route of quality and continuous improvement with a drive towards excellence based on employee participation. In contrast, SOX focuses on explicit regulations and punitive measures to address the lack of fiscal and accounting discipline in organizations. SOX is driven by compliance for fiscal management and reporting, while ISO 9001 is driven by customer focus and continuous improvement.

Chapter Summary

The Project Manager is on a mission to complete the project and move on to the next one. This mission can only be successful when the Project Manager genuinely embraces associated obligations as a professional, and strives to meet the intent and the spirit of the standards, processes and the law. Failure to recognize these obligations will jeopardize successful outcomes for organizations and their projects, and compromise the credibility of the Project Manager.

Learning Lessons

Avoid the Rat Hole – Warning Signs

1. There are no formal standards and processes for managing projects

2. The organization abandons the old methodology and adopts a new one frequently

3. The methodology is used as an excuse to justify project delays, overruns and failures

4. Everyone declares support for standards and methodology, but no one is willing to "walk the talk"

5. The Project Manager is experiencing difficulty balancing loyalties and obligations

Catch the "Pot of Gold" - Best Practices

1. Adopt a process-based methodology and stick to it

2. Conduct methodology training for the project team, clients and stakeholders

3. Provide executive orientation regarding project management, process improvement and regulatory compliance

4. Continually monitor your obligations as a Project Manager

5. Ask for help when faced with situations that may result in compromising one's integrity

17 finish the job with the right tools

The Project Manager's Tool Kit

"Give us the tools and we will finish the job"
- Winston Churchill

A project headed for a rat hole oscillates like a pendulum between two danger zones – FUBB and FUBR. That's Fouled Up Beyond Belief and Fouled Up Beyond Repair. Either of those situations will result in low morale, burn out, distrust, damaging stress and destructive conflicts leading to project failure.

A project that is not actively managed has a tendency to drift toward danger zones leading to the rat hole. As projects go down rat holes, so goes the morale and the reputation of the organization down the drain. The Project Manager's challenge is to manoeuvre the project and steer it skillfully to avoid danger zones, and achieve the intended project outcome.

The outstanding Project Manager makes a habit of continually scanning the horizon for a complete perspective and adjusts the plan accordingly. This is accomplished by making effective and judicious use of the tools of the trade, just like the basic tools used in any other profession, and applying Project Management skills.

The TEN Basic Tools

The ten basic tools of the Project Management profession are essentially pieces of documentation that help navigate the project successfully and prevent it from falling into a rat hole. *If you are not using the ten basic tools for Project Management, then what exactly are you using?*

If you don't have the tools or don't know how to use them, then you are probably spending most of your time managing a potentially run-away project and you may not even know about it. The tools, as described in the previous chapters, are summarized in Figure 17. Catch the Pot of Gold with the Project Manager's tools by exercising critical skills, and *Communicate, Communicate, Communicate!*

Figure 17

The TEN Tools of the Trade for Managing Successful Projects

1. Business Case & Project Charter
2. Project Organization Chart
3. Work Breakdown Structure
4. Dependency Chart & Critical Path
5. Major Milestones, Work Packages, Deliverables & Updated Schedule
6. RACI Chart (Responsibility Matrix)
7. Risk Assessment & Risk Plan (Top 3 Risks)
8. Financial Plan with the Six Measures (TBC, CBC, CAC, CEV, ETC, VAR)
9. Change Order Requests (Most Critical)
10. Status Reports, Issues & Escalations

Communicate .....Communicate .....Communicate!
If you are not using these, then what exactly are you using to manage your project?

The Power of Making It Visible

The fundamental principle of Project Management is to make the process, progress and problems visible so that everyone associated with the project is on the same page and corrective actions can be taken on a timely basis. Visual management is the way to accomplish this and it is a powerful approach for conveying a vast amount of information about the project. Project Managers rely on visual media such as charts, tools and presentations that help us to focus on a common goal, eliminate ambiguity, promote common understanding, facilitate communication and motivate the team to perform at its peak.

The WBS, Project Organization, Dependency, RACI and Cost Summary charts are not intended to be produced and filed away, but to be prominently displayed in the project area. When you display the charts, everyone knows what everyone else is doing on the project, and becomes more aware of their inter-dependencies. Displaying the charts also serves as a subtle, but powerful way of getting people to acknowledge their responsibilities and commitments. Remember, a picture is worth a thousand words!

Learning Lessons

Avoid the Rat Holes – Warning Signs

It is the responsibility of the Project Manager to recognize issues, escalate them and recommend solutions. Blaming issues on someone else and not doing anything about it is not an option.

In most cases, the failure of projects can be traced to the human element somewhere along the way. What appears as a technology failure is often a human and communication failure. Some of the most serious causes of failure manifest themselves in organizations in the following ways:

1. Culture of fear and intimidation - Nobody wants to tell the truth

2. Unrealistic and unachievable goals – Project team doesn't believe in them

3. Organizational resistance to change – Users don't see the benefits

4. Over reliance on sub-contractors – Abdicating responsibility for managing sub-contractors

5. Dissatisfied stakeholders – Lack of cooperation and commitment

6. User resistance to change - No buy-in from the user community

7. Down playing project risks - Ignorance of risks and risk management

8. Change Orders manage the project – Ill-defined requirements

9. Finger pointing among key players - Lack of trust and communication especially among engineering/ technology professionals and business functions

10. Dysfunctional management – Lack of management priorities or ineffective sponsorship

Catch the Rainbow – Best Practices

Customer Focus Counts

The sole purpose of a project is to satisfy the client's business and organizational goals and needs. Extraordinary Project Managers go beyond managing projects merely to the client's stated requirements. They focus on understanding their customers' needs, business rationale, desired outcomes and success criteria. They demonstrate the flexibility required to adapt to the client's changing business environment. Above all, they work with the customer to build a strong working relationship dedicated to achieving success in their projects. The customer comes first!

Sponsorship Leads to Success

Projects need an enthusiastic and committed sponsor to be successful. The sponsor sets the vision, ensures that the project is aligned with the business strategy, and provides organizational support for the Project Manager. Without this support, the Project

Manager faces immense challenges in overcoming organizational issues and resistance that are normally associated with a project.

The Project Manager's job is to get the project done, not change the organization or its culture (unless that in itself is within the scope of the project). The sponsor indicates true evidence of management's commitment to the project. Why undertake the project if management isn't serious about it? When it comes to managing successful projects, sponsorship does matter.

Relationships Are Rewarding

Every Project Manager aspires towards building a "trusted partner" relationship with clients and stakeholders including vendors, suppliers and sub-contractors. Relationships are crucial to exercising influence and arriving at decisions based on confidence, cooperation and consensus.

Good relationships help us build bridges with others at the emotional level where, in the final analysis, people tend to make most of their decisions. Such relationships thrive on mutual trust based on honesty and integrity. Experienced Project Managers practice an inclusive approach to project management by having the stakeholders' representation in project teams. Building strong relationships has its own rewards for Project managers.

Teams Thrive on Teamwork

Every project is an interesting and challenging endeavour in terms of getting work done with the active and enthusiastic participation of team members. Teams need to be structured and motivated and, most importantly, driven by a mission or purpose. Teamwork needs to be sustained by leadership that builds on, and promotes mutual respect, responsibility for accomplishment, sense of ownership and empowerment, and genuine recognition and unwavering trust among its members.

The hallmarks of a successful project are a sense of purpose, outstanding teamwork, mutual trust and a feeling of achievement. Project Managers provide leadership to create and build effective teams.

Process Improvement Pays

Just like any other work, Project Management can also be viewed as a series of processes. The processes define how an organization manages its project-related business including the use of standards, definition of phases, delivery of tasks, assessment of risks, and the conduct of management reporting, reviews and approvals.

The quality concept of Supplier, Input, Process, Output and Customer (SIPOC) is as much applicable to Project management processes as it is to any other work process. Project Management entails managing these processes with a focus on the customer and continuous improvement. Adopt a process view of Project Management, analyze and improve the processes, and win with successful projects!

Successful Project Management is built on a solid foundation of customer focus, executive sponsorship, organizational relationships, motivated teams and process orientation.

Build your foundation and catch the pot of gold!

appendix

Getting Work Done:
The Human Side of Project Management
A Checklist for Assessing Project Management Maturity

Project Management is defined as the art and science of getting work done with the active cooperation of individuals and organizations who are directly or indirectly involved with the project. This includes Senior Management, Project Sponsors(s), Customers, End-users, Stakeholders, Team Members, Sub-contractors, Vendors and Consultants.

Given the reality of minimal authority and total responsibility for the outcome of the project, the Project Manager's biggest challenge consist of "Getting Work Done".

Professional Project Management today is subject to increased industry pressures from accelerated implementations, restructuring and downsizing, mergers and acquisitions, faster technology obsolescence, and the use of new and unproven technologies. Furthermore, the project environment itself is rapidly changing with the use of distributed and virtual teams as organizations implement new "Projectized" cultures.

The Challenge for the Project Manager consists of attracting the right resources, forming a cohesive team, keeping the team motivated, meeting individual aspirations and getting the work done – all within scope, cost, time, and customer satisfaction! How should we meet the challenge of dealing with the human side of Project Management?

Here is a checklist with the "**Ten Golden Rules**" to help you assess the maturity level of Project Management and team effectiveness in your projects. Place a check mark against each question, only if you can answer it with a confident "Yes".

Golden Rule # 1:   Develop a Project Organization

☐ Are there specific individuals who are identified as the Sponsor and the Customer or Client for the project?

☐ Does everyone know who has the single source of responsibility for the project?

☐ Is there a Project Organization Chart with individuals identified for each role including team members and internal/external stakeholders?

☐ Are the roles, responsibilities and expectations clearly defined for each individual?

☐ Have the responsibilities and commitments been formally accepted by the individuals?

Golden Rule # 2:   Formulate a Team Purpose

☐ Is there a common understanding of project objectives and deliverables among all players?

☐ Are the "Vision, Purpose, Goals" of the project documented and supported by a scope definition with SMART objectives (i.e. Specific, Measurable, Achievable, Realistic and Target-driven)?

☐ Is there an agreed baseline schedule with resource commitments and intermediate milestones and deliverables for the project?

☐ Are the functional organizations that are impacted by the project on board with the project objectives and project plans?

☐ Did team members have input into the norms, rules and processes to be followed for smooth functioning of the team?

Golden Rule # 3:   Scope and Sell the Project

☐ Do you know who your clients are and do you have their enthusiastic support?

☐ Do you have a presentation that explains the business benefits of the project, its major components, how the project will be implemented and why it takes as long as it does?

☐ Do you have a Risk Management plan that you can execute if and when a major risk event occurs?

☐ Do you keep your client(s) positively engaged in the project and hold regular update/review meetings with your client(s) and project team?

☐ Does the Project Sponsor understand the complexity of the project and support the Project Manager in resolving problems that are outside his/her control?

Golden Rule # 4:   Insulate Team from Management Issues

☐ Is there a process for escalating problems to management and resolving issues?

☐ Is "Project Politics" practiced in a positive way to advance the project towards its completion and influence the intended project outcome?

☐ Is the Project Manager experience/trained to effectively delegate work, coach and support the team?

☐ Is the Project Manager experienced in exercising various communication tools and soft skills?

☐ Is there a well defined process for decision-making within the project team and is the process working?

Golden Rule # 5:   Teams Optimize, Individuals Maximize

☐ Does every team member clearly understand his/her deliverables, acceptance criteria, and the individuals who will be approving or accepting the deliverable?

☐ Is there an agreed facilitation process for team discussion and issue resolution?

☐ Are decisions arising from team meetings based on a decision making process primarily driven by consensus?

☐ Are the team members excited about the project experience? Do they see it as a learning opportunity for improving their competency, knowledge and skills?

☐ Is there a regularly published newsletter to communicate project and team achievements to all clients, stakeholders and the project team?

Golden Rule # 6:   Encourage & Facilitate Open Communication

☐ Is there a formal and structured communication process in place consisting of reviews, status reports, minutes of meetings and management updates etc.?

☐ Does the Communication Plan include weekly "One on One" reviews with team members?

☐ Does the review process allow for discussion of potential problems & possible solutions?

☐ Does the team environment genuinely believe in and encourage sharing and trust-building?

☐ Do team members believe that the team is empowered to make decisions relevant to how the work is to be done (as opposed to being micro-managed)?

Golden Rule # 7:   Institutionalize Positive Mindset

☐ Do your team members believe that their meetings are generally productive?

☐ Do you invite team members to provide feedback on the content and process of the meeting so that you can continually improve the management and performance of meetings?

☐ Are meeting participants willing to interact and listen effectively during your project meetings?

☐ Do your meetings focus on problem resolution as opposed to assignment of blame?

☐ Do you proactively ascertain the confidence & commitment of team members regularly?

Golden Rule # 8:   Remember the Five "R"s

☐ Does the project team practice and follow through the 5Rs - Respect, Recognition, Rewards, Rest and Recreation?

☐ Is the project baseline schedule realistic and based on reasonable assumptions?

☐ Do the team members believe that the project goal is both challenging and achievable?

☐ Do you celebrate significant achievements and milestones throughout the project life cycle?

- ☐ Do you formally thank, congratulate & recognize team members for their specific contribution on the project?

Golden Rule # 9:   Implement Consistent & Predictable Processes

- ☐ Are team members trained in the fundamentals of Project Management and are they familiar with the organization's business terminology and Project Management Methodology?

- ☐ Do team members clearly understand the differences and context of the various methodologies used for project management, system design, systems development, proprietary solutions and IT operations etc.?

- ☐ Is there a clear understanding of work packages, milestones, critical path and related project dependencies among the team members?

- ☐ Are team members trained to provide meaningful, clear & concise weekly status report?

- ☐ Do team members have the opportunity to develop their communication and soft skills as part of the project experience?

Golden Rule # 10:   Transition the Team Graciously

- ☐ Do you get a formal signoff from the client whenever a project deliverable is approved and accepted?

- ☐ Do you take the time to provide feedback to team members on their project performance?

- ☐ Do team members know their responsibilities with respect to Change Requests, Enhancements, Support, Warranty and Maintenance regarding the project deliverables.

- ☐ Do you hold formal debrief sessions including a post-implementation "Lessons Learnt" review with the team following project completion?

- ☐ Will your team members enthusiastically volunteer to be a part of your next project?

Score & Assess your Project Management and Team Building Skills

The questionnaire is intended for use by individuals, project teams, departments or organizations to measure the effectiveness of team work. Check your score by counting "Yes" responses to the questions and refer to the guideline below for assessment of the team building maturity level in your project organization.

What's your final score?

Total Score	Team Building Maturity Level	Team Building Maturity Assessment
1-10	*Initial* Level 1	No processes for Project Mgt. and team building; Working mostly on an "Ad-hoc" basis
11-20	*Repeatable* Level 2	Basic formal processes developed and used consistently for team building
21-30	*Defined* Level 3	Demonstrated mgt. support and processes for Project Management and team building
31-40	*Managed* Level 4	Evolving towards a "Projectized" culture and empowered high performance teams
41-50	*Optimizing* Level 5	Implemented self-managed High Performance Teams in a fully "Projectized" environment

If it is in the low tens, then you have a dysfunctional team and your project is certainly in a rathole. However, don't despair! Pray for a competent Project Manager to rescue the situation. Most projects start that way and evolve into a mature team with the Project Manager's organizational team building skills.

If your score is in the 20's, you can claim to have an "average team" and expect normal challenges in delivering your project. Most of the project teams based on my survey fall into this range.

A score in the mid-30's range indicates that the team is passionate and excited about the project, and is working smoothly, If you scored anything like mid-40's, then you are walking on water, and that's a dream come true for all Project Managers!

Conclusion

Creating successful teams requires conscious and deliberate investment of time and effort. Teams are built around four basic principles that recognize the importance of Team Structure, Team Process, Team Culture and Team Influence.

Team Structure provides leadership and organization. Process provides discipline and predictability for team interaction. Culture provides foundation for the team's norms and values for successful interdependence and relationships. Influence helps the team to leverage internal and external politics in a constructive way to drive the project to a successful outcome.

Teams must embrace a common purpose, and develop and follow a set of common processes based on a set of values and culture adopted by the team. The Project Manager's role in team building is to guide, coach, mentor, facilitate and direct as required to achieve the intended project outcome. The success and survival of project teams depends on understanding the human side of Project management.

bibliography & chapter references

Chapters 1 and 11: Project Management Institute. *Project Management Body of Knowledge (PMBOK).* Drexel Hill, PA: PMI Publication www.pmi.org

Chapters 1-17: Kothari, Dhanu. *The Twelve Windows of Project Management.* Markham, Canada: D2i Consulting 2004 www.D2i.ca

Chapter 1: Kothari, Dhanu. *Guest Editorial, Canadian Information Processing Society (CIPS) publication.* Toronto 1993. Excerpts printed with permission from CIPS.

Chapters 2 and 10: Mitchell, Romeo. *Project Management Workbooks* developed for the Project Management Certificate Program, Humber College, Toronto, Canada

Chapter 13: Geraats, Bill. *The Bridge Game for Team Building.* Markham, Canada: Vista Learning Services. www.bridgegame.com

Chapter 13: Kothari, Dhanu. *Managing and Motivating Teams* - Presentations to PMI Chapters

Chapter 14: Aranda, Eileen and Aranda, Luis. *TEAMS - Structure, Process, Culture and Politics.*

Chapter 15: Conference Board of Canada. *Project Management Skills & Competencies.* Ottawa, Canada: www.conferenceboard.ca

Chapter 15: Christopher Leadership Course. *Confidence!* www.christophers.org

Chapter 15: The Toronto Star. *Survey of email use among executives.* Toronto: January 2006

recommended reading

1. Albrecht, Karl. *Social Intelligence – The New Science of Success*. San Francisco: Jossey-Bass (Wiley) 2006 ISBN 0-7879-7938-4

2. Aranda, Eileen and Aranda, Luis. *TEAMS - Structure, Process, Culture and Politics.* New Jersey: Prentice Hall 1998 ISBN 0-13-494584-0

3. Barkley, Bruce and Saylor, James. *Customer-Driven Project Management*. New York: McGraw-Hill 2000 ISBN 0-07-136982-1

4. Block, Robert. *The Politics of Projects*. New Jersey: Prentice Hall 1983 ISBN 0-13-685553-9

5. Brooks, Frederick. *The Mythical Man Month* – Essays on Software Engineering. Massachusetts: Addison-Wesley 1978 ISBN 0-201-00650-2

6. Christopher Leadership Course. *Confidence!* New York: The Lumen Institute 1996

7. Craig, Malcolm. *Thinking Visually*. New York: Continuum 2000 ISBN 0-8264-4833-X

8. Hooks, Ivy and Farry, Kristin. *Customer-Centred Products* – Creating Successful Products through Smart Requirements Management. New York: American Management Association 2001 ISBN 0-8144-0568-1

9. Jalote, Pankaj. *Software Project management in Practice.* Addison-Wesley (Pearson Education) 2000 ISBN 0201737213

10. Kothari, Dhanu and Mitchell, Romeo. *From Ratholes to Rainbows:* Managing Project Recovery"

11. Leeds, Dorothy. *The Seven Powers of Questions.* New York: Berkley Publishing 2000 ISBN 0-399-52614-5

12. Liker, Jeffrey. *The Toyota Way.* New York: McGraw Hill 2004 ISBN 0-07-139231-9

13. Murphy, James. *Flawless Execution.* New York: Harper Collins 2005 ISBN 0-06-076049-4

14. Project Management Institute. *A Guide to the Project Management Body of Knowledge.* Pennsylvania: Project Management Institute 2000 ISBN 1-880410-23-0

15. Scholtes, Peter, Joiner, Brian and Streibel, Barbara. *The TEAM Handbook.* Wisconsin: Oriel Publications 2003 ISBN 1-884731-26-0

16. Summers, Donna. *Quality Management – Creating and Sustaining Organizational Effectiveness.* New Jersey: Pearson Prentice Hall 2005 ISBN 0-13-262643-8

index

Acceptor	16,71,82
Accomplish	7,17,28,59,72,88,96,111,151,165,166
Authority-PM's	13-18,81-83,87-90,135,171
Baseline	27-32,42,64,69,72-74,103,106,110,117,172
Best Practices	11,18,25,33,44,54,65,79,90,102,113,126,134,143,153, 163,168
Bus. Alignment	17,22-24
Business Case	19,20,25
Client Mgr.	50,54,71,98
Cost Planning & Cost Measures	6,7,19,20,27,103-113
Critical Path	7,57-65,72,73,86,130,176
Debriefing	123,124,177
Decision Making	99,130,134,146,149,174
Deliverables	8,9,29,36,38-43,50,54,59,70,73-77,82,84-86,89,111, 116, 119,125,126,157,172
Dependency	29,57-62,70,72,143,167
End Users	23,46,52,122
Governance	160-161
ISO 9001	118,162
Lead Designer	45,48
Methodology	4,51,67-69,118,160-163,176
Mgt. Support	20,23,130
Micro-mgt.	41,88,89,131,175
Milestone	7,29,32,58-60,63-65,70,72,74,81,86,89,111,124, 130-131,143,172,175

People Mgt.	13-17,36,40,127-134,140,141
PM Loyalties	48,135,141,155-158,163
Politics	46,47,51,53,83,86,89,123,130,141,158,173
Proj. Champion	46,50,51
Proj. Mgr. Role	48
Proj. Sponsor	5,6,19,24,45,47,53,71,100,129,168,169,173
Project Defn.	5-7
Project Mgr. Responsibility	7-11,48
Project Org.	7,45-54,69,71,100,122,129,143,167,172,177
Project Plan	67-79
Project Team	40,45,48,51-52,127-134,158,169
Quality	6,9,70,75-76,93,115-126,162,170
RACI Chart	59,76,84-90
Rationale	21,25,63,71,117,168
Risk Mgt.	8,21,27,70,75,93-101
Roadmap	57-65,76
ROI	19,20,24,25,108
Roles & Resp.	17,45-54
Scope	6,7,21,23,25,27,35-43
Skills–PM	5,17,18,42
Soft Skills	133,145-153,173,176
SOX Act	158-162
Stakeholders	8,13,41-48, 54,77,82,90,96-100,124,129,133-135,150,155,158,160,163,168-172

Steering Comm.	45-47, 71
TIMO Risk Mgt.	96,101,102
Tools & Toolkit for PM	15,28,33,42,67-69,75,76,84,96,117,119-126,132, 135-137,142,149,164-165
Warning Signs	11,17,25,33,43,53,64,78,90,101,112,125,134,142,152, 163,167
WBS - Work Breakdown	25,35,38-44,70,72,104,107,167

Printed in January 2009
at Gauvin Press,
Gatineau, Québec